Progressive Morality

Thomas Fowler

Contents

PREFACE. 7
CHAPTER I. INTRODUCTION. THE SANCTIONS OF CONDUCT. 8
CHAPTER II. THE MORAL SANCTION OR MORAL SENTIMENT. ....
    ITS FUNCTIONS AND THE JUSTIFICATION OF ITS CLAIMS ....
    TO SUPERIORITY. 16
CHAPTER III. ANALYSIS AND FORMATION OF THE MORAL ....
    SENTIMENT. ITS EDUCATION AND IMPROVEMENT. 22
CHAPTER IV. THE MORAL TEST AND ITS JUSTIFICATION. 39
CHAPTER V. PRACTICAL APPLICATIONS OF THE MORAL TEST. 61

PROGRESSIVE MORALITY

BY

Thomas Fowler

PREFACE.

These pages represent an attempt to exhibit a scientific conception of morality in a popular form, and with a view to practical applications rather than the discussion of theoretical difficulties. For this purpose it has been necessary to study brevity and avoid controversy. Hence, I have made few references to other authors, and I have almost altogether dispensed with foot-notes. But, though I have attempted to state rather than to defend my views, I believe that they are, in the main, those which, making exception for a few back eddies in the stream of modern thought, are winning their way to general acceptance among the more instructed and reflective men of our day.

It is necessary that I should state that this Essay is independent of a much larger work, entitled the 'Principles of Morals,' on which I was, some years ago, engaged with my predecessor, the late Professor Wilson. Owing to the declining state of his health during the latter years of his life, that work was, at the time of his death, left in a condition which rendered its completion very difficult and its publication probably undesirable. For the present work I am solely responsible, though no one can have been brought into close contact with so powerful a mind as that of Professor Wilson, without deriving from it much stimulus and retaining many traces of its influence.

It has long been my belief that the questions of theoretical Ethics would be far less open to dispute, as well as far more intelligible, if they were considered with more direct reference to practice. This little book will, I trust, furnish an example, however slight and imperfect, of such a mode of treatment.

C.C.C.
July 25, 1884.

CHAPTER I.
INTRODUCTION. THE SANCTIONS OF CONDUCT.

All reflecting men acknowledge that both the theory and the practice of morality have advanced with the general advance in the intelligence and civilisation of the human race. But, if this be so, morality must be a matter capable of being reasoned about, a subject of investigation and of teaching, in which the less intelligent members of a community have always something to learn from the more intelligent, and the more intelligent, in their turn, have ever fresh problems to solve and new material to study. It becomes, then, of prime importance to every educated man, to ask what are the data of Ethics, what is the method by which its general principles are investigated, what are the considerations which the moralist ought to apply to the solution of the complex difficulties of life and action. And still, in spite of these obvious facts, ethical investigation, or any approach to an independent review of the current morality, is always unpopular with the great mass of mankind. Though the conduct of their own lives is the subject which most concerns men, it is that in which they are least patient of speculation. Nothing is so wounding to the self-complacency of a man of indolent habits of mind as to call in question any of the moral principles on which he habitually acts. Praise and blame are usually apportioned, even by educated men, according to vague and general rules, with little or no regard to the individual circumstances of the case. And of all innovators, the innovator on ethical theory is apt to be the most unpopular and to be the least able to secure impartial attention to his speculations. And hence it is that vague theories, couched in unintelligible or only half-intelligible language, and almost totally inapplicable to practice, have usually done duty for what is called a system of moral philosophy. The authors or exponents of such theories have the good fortune at once to avoid odium and to acquire a reputation for profundity.

In the following pages, I shall attempt (1) to discriminate morality, properly so called, from other sanctions of conduct; (2) to determine the precise functions, and the ultimate justification, of the moral sentiment, or, in other words, of the moral sanction; (3) to enquire how this sentiment has been formed, and how it may be further educated and improved; (4) to discover some general test of conduct; (5) to give examples of the application of this test to existing moral rules and moral feelings, with a view to shew how far they may be justified and how far they require extension or reformation. As my subject is almost exclusively practical, I shall studiously avoid mere theoretical puzzles, such as is pre-eminently that of the freedom of the will, which, in whatever way resolved, probably never influences, and never will influence, any sane man's conduct. Questions of this kind will always excite interest in the sphere of speculation, and speculation is a necessity of the cultivated human intellect; but it does not seem to me that they can be profitably discussed in a treatise, the aim of which is simply to suggest principles for examining, for testing, and, if possible, for improving the prevailing sentiment on matters of practical morals.

To begin with the first division of my subject, How is morality, properly so called, discriminated from other sanctions of conduct? By a sanction I may premise that I mean any pleasure which attracts to as well as any pain which deters from a given course of action. In books on Jurisprudence, this word is usually employed to designate merely pains or penalties, but this circumstance arises from the fact that, at least in modern times, the law seldom has recourse to rewards, and effects its ends almost exclusively by means of punishments. When we are considering conduct, however, in its general aspects and not exclusively in its relations to law, we appear to need a word to express any inducement, whether of a pleasureable or painful nature, which may influence a man's actions, and such a word the term 'sanction' seems conveniently to supply. Taking the word in this extended sense, the sanctions of conduct may be enumerated as the physical, the legal, the social, the religious, and the moral. Of the physical sanction familiar examples may be found in the headache from which a man suffers after a night's debauch, the pleasure of relaxation which awaits a well-earned holiday, the danger to life or limb which is attendant on reckless exercise, or the glow of constant satisfaction which rewards a healthy habit of life. These pleasures and pains, when once experienced, exercise, for the future, an attracting or a deterring influence, as the case may be, on the courses of conduct with which they have respectively become associated. Thus, a man who has once suffered from a severe headache, after a night's drinking-bout, will be likely to exercise more discretion in future, or the prospect of agreeable diversion, at the end of a hard day's work, will quicken a man's efforts to execute his task. The legal sanction is too familiar to need illustration. Without penal laws, no society of any size could exist for a day. There are, however, two characteristics of this sanction which it is important to point out. One is that it works almost exclusively[1] by means of penalties. It would be an endless and thankless business, in a society of any size, even if it were possible, to attempt to reward the virtuous for their consideration in not breaking the laws. The cheap, the effective, indeed, in most cases, the only possible method is to punish the transgressor. By a carefully devised and properly graduated system of penalties each citizen is thus furnished with the strongest inducement to refrain from those acts which may injure or annoy his neighbour. Another characteristic of the legal sanction is that, though it is professedly addressed to all citizens alike, it actually affects the uneducated and lower classes far more than the educated and higher classes of society. This circumstance arises partly from the fact that persons in a comfortable position of life are under little temptation to commit the more ordinary crimes forbidden by law, such as are theft, assault, and the like, and partly from the fact that their education and associations make them more amenable to the social, and, in most cases, to the moral and religious sanctions, about to be described presently. Few persons in what are called the higher or middle ranks of life have any temptation to commit, say, an act of theft, and, if they experienced any such temptation, they would be at least as likely to be restrained by the consideration of what their neighbours would think or say about them, even apart from their own moral and religious convictions, as by the fear of imprisonment.

One of the most effective sanctions in all conditions of life, but especially in the upper and better educated circles of a civilized society, is what may be called the

---

1 There are a few exceptions to the rule that the sanctions employed by the state assume the form of punishments rather than of rewards. Such are titles and honours, pensions awarded for distinguished service, rewards to informers, &c. But these exceptions are almost insignificant, when compared with the numerous examples of the general rule.

social sanction, that is to say, a regard for the good opinion and a dread of the evil opinion of those who know us, and especially of those amongst whom we habitually live. It is one of the characteristics of this sanction that it is much more far-reaching than the legal sanction. Not only does it extend to many acts of a moral character which are not affected, in most countries, by the legal sanction, such as lying, backbiting, ingratitude, unkindness, cowardice, but also to mere matters of taste or fashion, such as dress, etiquette, and even the proprieties of language. Indeed, as to the latter class of actions, there is always considerable danger of the social sanction becoming too strong. Society is apt to insist on all men being cast in one mould, without much caring to examine the character of the mould which it has adopted. And it frequently happens that a wholly disproportionate value thus comes to be attached to the observance of mere rules of etiquette and good-breeding as compared with acts and feelings which really concern the moral and social welfare of mankind. There is many a man, moving in good society, who would rather be guilty of, and even detected in, an act of unkindness or mendacity, than be seen in an unfashionable dress or commit a grammatical solecism or a broach of social etiquette. Vulgarity to such men is a worse reproach than hardness of heart or indifferent morality. In these cases, as we shall see hereafter, the social sanction requires to be corrected by the moral and religious sanctions, and it is the special province of the moral and religious teacher in each generation to take care that this correction shall be duly and effectively applied. The task may, from time to time, require the drastic hand of the moral or religious reformer, but, unless some one has the courage to undertake it, we are in constant danger of neglecting the weightier matters of the law, while we are busy with the mint and cummin and anise of fashion and convention. But, notwithstanding the danger of exaggeration and misapplication, there can be no doubt of the vast importance and the generally beneficial results of a keen sensitiveness to the opinions of our fellow-men. Without the powerful aid of this sanction, the restraints of morality and religion would often be totally ineffective.

When the social sanction operates, not through society generally, but through particular sections of society, it may be called a Law of Honour, a term which originated in the usages of Chivalry. In a complex and civilized form of society, such as our own, there may be many such laws of honour, and the same individual may be subject to several of them. Thus each profession, the army, the navy, the clerical, the legal, the medical, the artistic, the dramatic profession, has its own peculiar code of honour or rules of professional etiquette, which its members can only infringe on pain of ostracism, or, at least, of loss of professional reputation. The same is the case with trades, and is specially exemplified in the instance of trades-unions, or, their mediaeval prototypes, the guilds. A college or a school, again, has its own rules and traditions, which the tutor or undergraduate, the master or boy, can often only violate at his extreme peril. Almost every club, institution, and society affords another instance in point. The class of 'gentlemen,' too, that is to say, speaking roughly, the upper and upper middle ranks of society, claim to have a code of honour of their own, superior to that of the ordinary citizen. A breach of this code is called 'ungentlemanly' rather than wrong or immoral or unjust or unkind. So far as this code insists on courtesy of demeanour and delicacy of feeling and conduct, it is a valuable complement to the ordinary rules of morality, though, so far as it fulfils this function, it plainly ought not to be the exclusive possession of one class, but ought to be communicated, by means of example and education, to the classes who are now supposed to be bereft of it. There are points in this code, however, such as that the payment of 'debts of honour' should take precedence of that of tradesmen's bills, and that less courtesy is due to persons in an inferior station than to those in our own, which at least merit re-consideration. It may, indeed, be said of all these laws or codes of honour, that, though they have probably, on the whole, a salutary effect in maintaining a high standard of conduct in the various bodies or classes where they obtain, they require to be constantly watched, lest they should become capricious or tyrannical, and specially lest they should conflict with the wider interests of society or the deeper instincts of morality. It must not be forgotten that we are 'men' before we are 'gentlemen,' and that no claims of any profession, institution, or class can replace or supplant those of humanity and citizenship.

We see, then, or rather we are obliged at the present stage of our enquiry to assume, that the social sanction, whether it be derived from the average sentiment of society at large or from the customs and opinions of particular aggregates of society, requires constant correction at the hands of the moralist. The sentiment which it represents may be only the sentiment of men of average moral tone, or it may even be that of men of an inferior or degraded morality, and hence it often needs to be tested by the application of rules derived from a higher standard both of feeling and intelligence. Nor is it the moral standard only which may be used to correct the social standard. We may often advantageously have recourse to the legal standard for the same purpose. For the laws of a country express, as a rule, the sentiments of the wisest and most experienced of its citizens, and hence we might naturally expect that they would be in advance of the average moral sentiment of the people, as well as of the social traditions of particular professions or classes. And this I believe to be usually the case. For instances, we have to go no further than the comparison between the laws and the popular or professional sentiment on bribery at elections, on smuggling, on evasion of taxation, on fraudulent business transactions, on duelling, on prize-fighting, or on gambling. At the same time it must be confessed that, as laws sometimes become antiquated, and the leanings of lawyers are proverbially conservative, it occasionally happens that, on some points, the average moral sentiment is in advance of the law. I may select as examples, from comparatively recent legal history, the continuance of religious disabilities and the excessive punishment of ordinary or even trivial crimes; and, perhaps, I may venture to add, as a possible reform in the future now largely demanded by popular sentiment, some considerable modifications of the laws regulating the transfer of and the succession to landed property. Thus it will be seen that law and the sentiment of society may each be employed as corrective of the other, and that, consequently, their comparison implies a higher standard than either, by means of which each may be tested, and to which each, in its turn, may be referred. This higher or common standard it will be our business to consider in a subsequent part of this Essay. Meanwhile, it may be pointed out that, in addition to its function as an occasional corrective of the legal sanction, the social sanction subserves two great objects: first, it largely complements the legal sanction, being applicable to numberless cases which that sanction does not, and, in fact, cannot reach; secondly, the legal sanction, even in those cases which it reaches, is greatly reinforced by the social sanction, which adds the pains arising from an evil reputation, and all the indefinable social inconveniences which an evil reputation brings with it, to the actual penalties inflicted by the law.

The religious sanction varies, of course, with the different religious creeds, and, in the more imperfect forms of religion, by no means always operates in favour of morality. But it will be sufficient here to consider the religious sanction solely in relation to Christianity. As enforced by the Bible and the Church, the religious sanctions of conduct are two, which I shall call the higher and the lower sanctions. By the latter I mean the hope of the divine reward or the fear of the divine punishment, either in this world or the next; by the former, the love of God and that veneration for His nature which irresistibly inspires the effort to imitate His perfections. The lower religious sanction is plainly the same in kind with the legal sanction. If a man is induced to do or to refrain from doing a certain action from fear of punishment, the motive is the same, whether the punishment be for a long time or a short one, whether it is to take immediate effect or to be deferred for a term of years. And, similarly, the same is the case with rewards. No peculiar merit, as it appears to me, can be claimed by a man because he acts from fear of divine punishment rather than of human punishment, or from hope of divine rewards rather than of human rewards. The only differences between the two sanctions are (1) that the hopes and fears inspired by the religious sanction are, to one who believes in their reality, far more intense than those inspired by the legal sanction, the two being related as the temporal to the eternal, and (2) that, inasmuch as God is regarded as omnipresent and omniscient, the religious sanction is immeasurably more far-reaching than the legal sanction or even than the legal and the social sanctions combined. Thus the lower religious sanction is, to those who really believe in it, far more effective than the legal sanction, though it is the same in kind. But the higher religious sanction appeals to a totally different class of motives, the motives of love and reverence rather than of hope and fear. In this higher frame of mind, we keep God's commandments, because we love Him, not because we hope for His rewards or fear His punishments. We reverence God, and, therefore, we strive to be like Him, to be perfect even as He is perfect. We have attained to that state of mind in which perfect love has cast out fear, and, hence, we simply do good and act righteously because God, who is the supreme object of our love and the supreme ideal of conduct, is good and righteous. There can be no question that, in this case, the motives are far loftier and purer than in the case of the legal and the lower religious sanctions. But there are few men, probably, capable of these exalted feelings, and, therefore, for the great mass of mankind the external inducements to right conduct must, probably, continue to be sought in the coarser motives. It may be mentioned, before concluding this notice of the religious sanctions, that there is a close affinity between the higher religious sanction and that form of the social sanction which operates through respect for the good opinions of those of our fellow-men whom we love, reverence, or admire. But, quite distinct from all the sanctions thus far enumerated, there is another sanction which is derived from our own reflexion on our own actions, and the approbation or disapprobation which, after such reflexion, we bestow upon them. There are actions which, on no reasonable estimate of probabilities, can ever come to the knowledge of any other person than ourselves, but which we look back on with pleasure or regret. It may be said that, though, in these cases, the legal and the social sanctions are confessedly excluded, the sanction which really operates is the religious sanction, in either its higher or its lower form. But it can hardly be denied that, even where there is no belief in God, or, at least, no vivid sense of His presence nor any effective expectation of His intervention, the same feelings are experienced. These feelings, then, appear to be distinct in character from any of the others which we have so far considered, and they constitute what may appropriately be called the moral sanction, in the strict sense of the term. It is one of the faults of Bentham's system that he confounds this sanction with the social sanction, speaking indifferently of the moral *or* popular (that is to say, social) sanction; but let any one examine carefully for himself the feelings of satisfaction or dissatisfaction with which he looks back upon past acts of his own life, and ask himself whether he can discover in those feelings any reference to the praise or blame of other persons, actual or possible. There will, if I mistake not, be many of them in which he can discover no such reference, but in which the feeling is simply that of satisfaction with himself for having done what he ought to have done, or dissatisfaction with himself for having done that which he ought not to have done. Whether these feelings admit of analysis and explanation is another question, and one with which I shall deal presently, but of their reality and distinctness no competent and impartial person, on careful self-examination, can well doubt. The answer, then, to our first question, I conceive to be that the moral sanction, properly so called, is distinguished from all other sanctions of conduct in that it has no regard to the prospect of physical pleasure or pain, or to the hope of reward or fear of punishment, or to the estimation in which we shall be held by any other being than ourselves, but that it has regard simply and solely to the internal feeling of satisfaction or dissatisfaction with which, on reflexion, we shall look back upon our own acts.

CHAPTER II.
THE MORAL SANCTION OR MORAL SENTIMENT. ITS FUNCTIONS AND THE JUSTIFICATION OF ITS CLAIMS TO SUPERIORITY.

I now proceed to consider more at length what are the precise functions of the moral sentiment or moral sanction[2], and what is the justification of the weight which we attach to it, or rather of the preference which we assign to it, or feel that we ought to assign to it, over all the other sanctions of conduct. We have already seen that the moral sentiment or sanction is the feeling of satisfaction or dissatisfaction which we experience when we reflect on our own acts, without any reference to any external authority or external opinion. Now it is important

---

2 I use the expressions 'moral sanction' and 'moral sentiment' as equivalent terms, because the pleasures and pains, which constitute the moral sanction, are inseparable, even in thought, from the moral feeling. The moral feeling of self-approbation or self-disapprobation cannot even be conceived apart from the pleasures or pains which are attendant on it, and by means of which it reveals itself to us.

It should be noticed that the expression 'moral sentiment' is habitually used in two senses, as the equivalent (1) of the moral feeling only, (2) of the entire moral process, which, as we shall see in the third chapter, consists partly of a judgment, partly of a feeling. It is in the latter sense, for instance, that we speak of the 'current moral sentiment' of any given age or country, meaning the opinions then or there prevalent on moral questions, reinforced by the feeling of approbation or disapprobation. As, however, the moral feeling always follows immediately and necessarily on the moral judgment, whenever that judgment pronounces decisively for or against an action, and always implies a previous judgment (I am here again obliged to anticipate the discussion in chapter 3), the ambiguity is of no practical importance at the present stage of our enquiry. It is almost needless to add that the word 'sentiment,' when used alone, has the double meaning of a feeling and an opinion, an ambiguity which is sometimes not without practical inconvenience.

to ask whether this feeling is uniformly felt on the occurrence of the same acts, or whether it ever varies, so that acts, for instance, which are at one time viewed with satisfaction, are at another time regarded with indifference or with positive dissatisfaction. It would seem as if no man who reflects on ethical subjects, and profits by the observation and experience of life, could possibly answer this question in any other than one way. There must be very few educated and reflective men who have not seen reason, with advancing years, to alter their opinion on many of, at least, the minor points of morality in which they were instructed as children. A familiar instance occurs at once in the different way in which most of us view card-playing or attendance at balls or theatres from the much stricter views which prevailed in many respectable English households a generation ago. On the other hand, excess in eating and drinking is regarded with far less indulgence now than it was in the days of our fathers and grandfathers. On these points, then, at least, and such as these, it must be allowed that there is a variation of moral sentiment, or, in other words, that the acts condemned or approved by the moral sanction are not invariably the same. Moreover, any of us who are accustomed to reason on moral questions, and can observe carefully the processes through which the mind passes, will notice that there is constantly going on a re-adjustment, so to speak, of our ethical opinions, whether we are reviewing abstract questions of morality or the specific acts of ourselves or others. We at one time think ourselves or others more, and, at another time, less blameable for the self-same acts, or we come to regard some particular class of acts in a different light from what we used to do, either modifying our praise or blame, or, in extreme cases, actually substituting one for the other. But, though these facts are patent, and may be verified by any one in his experience either of himself or others, there have actually been moralists who have appeared to maintain the position that, when a man is unbiassed by passion or interest, his moral judgments are and must be invariably the same. This error has, undoubtedly, been largely fostered by the loose and popular use of the terms conscience and moral sense. These terms, and especially the word conscience, are often employed to designate a sort of mysterious entity, supposed to have been implanted in the mind by God Himself, and endowed by Him with the unique prerogative of infallibility. Even so philosophical and sober a writer as Bishop Butler has given some countenance to this extravagant supposition, and to the exaggerated language which he employs on the prerogatives of conscience, and to the emphatic manner in which he insists on the absolute, if not the infallible, character of its decisions, may be traced much of the misconception which still prevails on the subject. But we have only to take account of the notorious fact that the consciences of two equally conscientious men may point in entirely opposite directions, in order to see that the decisions of conscience cannot, at all events, be credited with infallibility. Those who denounce and those who defend religious persecution, those who insist on the removal and those who insist on the retention of religious disabilities, those who are in favour of and those who are opposed to a relaxation of the marriage laws, those who advocate a total abstention from intoxicating liquors and those who allow of a moderate use of them,--men on both sides in these controversies, or, at least, the majority of them, doubtless act conscientiously, and yet, as they arrive at opposite conclusions, the conscience of one side or other must be at fault. There is no act of religious persecution, there are few acts of political or personal cruelty, for which the authority of conscience might not be invoked. I doubt not that Queen Mary acted as conscientiously in burning the Reformers as they did in promulgating their opinions or we do in condemning her acts. It is plain, then, not only that the decisions of conscience are not infallible, but that they must, to a very large extent, be relative to the circumstances and opinions of those who form them. In any intelligible or tenable sense of the term, conscience stands simply for the aggregate of our moral opinions reinforced by the moral sanction of self-approbation or self-disapprobation. That we ought to act in accordance with these opinions, and that we are acting wrongly if we act in opposition to them, is a truism. 'Follow Conscience' is the only safe guide, when the moment of action has arrived. But it is equally important to insist on the fallibility of conscience, and to urge men, by all means in their power, to be constantly improving and instructing their consciences, or, in plain words, to review and, wherever occasion offers, to correct their conceptions of right and wrong. The 'plain, honest man' of Bishop Butler would, undoubtedly, always follow his conscience, but it is by no means certain that his conscience would always guide him rightly, and it is quite certain that it would often prompt him differently from the consciences of other 'plain, honest men' trained elsewhere and under other circumstances. To act contrary to our opinions of right and wrong would be treason to our moral nature, but it does not follow that those opinions are not susceptible of improvement and correction, or that it is not as much our duty to take pains to form true opinions as to act in accordance with our opinions when we have formed them.

The terms 'conscience' and 'moral sense' are very convenient expressions for popular use, provided we always bear in mind that 'illuminate' or 'instruct' your 'conscience' or 'moral sense' is quite as essential a rule as 'follow' your 'conscience' or 'moral sense.' But the scientific moralist, in attempting to analyse the springs of moral action and to detect the ultimate sanctions of conduct, would do well to avoid these terms altogether. The analysis of moral as well as of intellectual acts is often only obscured by our introducing the conception of 'faculties,' and, in the present instance, it is far better to confine ourselves to the expressions 'acts' of 'approbation or disapprobation,' 'satisfaction or dissatisfaction,' which we shall hereafter attempt to analyse, than to feign, or at least assume, certain 'faculties' or 'senses' as distinct entities from which such acts are supposed to proceed. I shall, therefore, in the sequel of this work, say little or nothing of 'conscience' or 'moral sense,' not because I think it desirable to banish those words from popular terminology, but because I think that, in an attempt to present the principles of ethics in a scientific form, they introduce needless complexity and obscurity.

If the statements thus far made in this chapter be accepted, it follows that the feelings of self-approbation and self-disapprobation, which constitute the moral sanction, by no means invariably supervene on acts of the same kind even in the case of the same individual, much less in the case of different individuals, and that the acts which elicit the moral sanction depend, to a considerable extent, on the circumstances and education of the person who passes judgment on them. The moral sanction, therefore, though it always consists in the feelings of self-approbation, or self-disapprobation, of satisfaction or dissatisfaction at one's own acts, is neither uniform, absolute, nor infallible; but varies, as applied not only by different individuals but by the same individual at different times, in relation to varying conditions of education, temperament, nationality, and, generally, of circumstances both external and internal. Lastly, it admits of constant improvement and correction. How, then, it may be asked, do we justify the application of this sanction, and why do we regard it as not only a legitimate sanction of conduct, but as the most important of all sanctions, and, in cases of conflict, the supreme and final sanction?

The answer to this question is that, if we regard an action as wrong, no matter whether our opinion be correct or not, no external considerations whatsoever can compensate us for acting contrary to our convictions. Human nature, in its normal condition, is so constituted that the remorse felt, when we look back upon a wrong action, far outweighs any pleasure we may have derived from it, just as the satisfaction with which we look back upon a right action far more than compensates for any pain with which it may have been attended. The 'mens sibi conscia recti' is the highest reward which a man can have, as, on the other hand, the retrospect on base, unjust, or cruel actions constitutes the most acute of torments. Now, when a man looks back upon his past actions, what he regards is not so much the result of his acts as the intention and the motives by which the intention was actuated. It is not, therefore, what he would now think of the act so much as what he then thought of it that is the object of his approbation or disapprobation. And, consequently, even though his opinions as to the nature of the act may meanwhile have undergone alteration, he approves or disapproves of what was his intention at the moment of performing it and of the state of mind from which it then proceeded. It is true that the subsequent results of our acts and any change in our estimate of their moral character may considerably modify the feelings with which we look back upon them, but, still, in the main, it holds good that the approval or disapproval with which we regard our past conduct depends rather upon the opinions of right and wrong which we entertained at the moment of action than those which we have come to entertain since. To have acted, at any time, in a manner contrary to what we then supposed to be right leaves behind it a trace of dissatisfaction and pain, which may, at any future time, reappear to trouble and distress us; just as to have acted, in spite of all conflicting considerations, in a manner which we then conceived to be right, may, in after years, be a perennial source of pleasure and satisfaction. It is characteristic of the pleasures and pains of reflexion on our past acts (which pleasures and pains of reflexion may, of course, connect themselves with other than purely moral considerations), not only that they admit of being more intense than any other pleasures and pains, but that, whenever there is any conflict between the moral sanction and any other sanction, it is to the moral sanction that they attach themselves. Thus, if a man has incurred physical suffering, or braved the penalties of the law or the ill word of society, in pursuance of a course of conduct which he deemed to be right, he looks back upon his actions with satisfaction, and the more important the actions, and the clearer his convictions of right and the stronger the inducements to act otherwise, the more intense will his satisfaction be. But no such satisfaction is felt, when a man has sacrificed his convictions of right to avoid physical pain, or to escape the penalties of the law, or to conciliate the goodwill of society; the feeling, on the other hand, will be that of dissatisfaction with himself, varying, according to circumstances, from regret to remorse. And, if no similar remark has to be made with reference to the religious sanction, it is because, in all the higher forms of religion, the religious sanction is conceived of as applying to exactly the same actions as the moral sanction. What a man himself deems right, that he conceives God to approve of, and what he conceives God as disapproving of, that he deems wrong. But in a religion in which God was not regarded as holy, just, and true, or in which there was a plurality of gods, some good and some evil, I conceive that a man would look back with satisfaction, and not with dissatisfaction, on those acts in which he had followed his own sense of right rather than the supposed will of the Deity, just as, when there is a conflict between the two, he now congratulates himself on having submitted to the claims of conscience rather than to those of the law.

The justification, then, of that claim to superiority, which is asserted by the moral sanction, consists, I conceive, in two circumstances: first, that the pleasures and pains, the feelings of satisfaction and dissatisfaction, of self-approbation and self-disapprobation, by means of which it works, are, in the normally constituted mind, far more intense and durable than any other pleasures and pains; secondly, that, whenever this sanction comes into conflict with any other sanction, its defeat is sure, on a careful retrospect of our acts, to bring regret or remorse, whereas its victory is equally certain to bring pleasure and satisfaction. We arrive, then, at the conclusion that it is the moral sanction which is the distinctive guide of conduct, and to which we must look, in the last resort, to enforce right action, while the other sanctions are mainly valuable in so far as they reinforce the moral sanction or correct its aberrations. A man must, ultimately, be the judge of his own conduct, and, as he acts or does not act according to his own best judgment, so he will subsequently feel satisfaction or remorse; but these facts afford no reason why he should not take pains to inform his judgment by all the means which physical knowledge, law, society, and religion place at his disposal.

CHAPTER III.
ANALYSIS AND FORMATION OF THE MORAL SENTIMENT. ITS EDUCATION AND IMPROVEMENT.

Before proceeding to our third question, namely, how the moral sentiment, which is the source of the moral sanction, has been formed, and how it may be further educated and improved, it is desirable to discriminate carefully between the intellectual and the emotional elements in an act of approbation or disapprobation. We sometimes speak of moral judgment, sometimes of moral feeling. These expressions ought not to be regarded as the symbols of rival theories on the nature of the act of moral approbation, as has sometimes been the case, but as designating distinct parts of the process, or, to put the same statement rather differently, separate elements in the analysis. Hume, whose treatment of this subject is peculiarly lucid, as compared with that of most writers on ethics, after reviewing the reasons assigned by those authors respectively who resolve the act of approbation into an act of judgment or an act of feeling, adds[3]: 'These arguments on each side (and many more might be produced) are so plausible, that I am apt to suspect they may, the one as well as the other, be solid and satisfactory, and that reason and sentiment concur in almost all moral determinations and conclusions. The final sentence; it is probable, which pronounces characters and actions amiable or odious, praiseworthy or blameable; that which stamps on them the mark of honour or infamy, approbation or censure; that which renders morality an active principle, and constitutes virtue our happiness and vice our misery: it is probable, I say, that this final sentence depends on some internal sense or feeling, which na-

---

3 Enquiry concerning the Principles of Morals, Section I

ture has made universal in the whole species. For what else can have an influence of this nature? But, in order to pave the way for such a sentiment and give a proper discernment of its object, it is often necessary, we find, that much reasoning should precede, that nice distinctions be made, just conclusions drawn, distant comparisons formed, complicated relations examined, and general facts fixed and ascertained. Some species of beauty, especially the natural kinds, on their first appearance, command our affection and approbation; and, where they fail of this effect, it is impossible for any reasoning to redress their influence, or adapt them better to our taste and sentiment. But in many orders of beauty, particularly those of the finer arts, it is requisite to employ much reasoning, in order to feel the proper sentiment; and a false relish may frequently be corrected by argument and reflexion. There are just grounds to conclude that moral beauty partakes much of this latter species, and demands the assistance of our intellectual faculties, in order to give it a suitable influence on the human mind.'

This passage, which I have thought it worth while to quote at length, exhibits, with sufficient clearness, the respective provinces of reason and feeling in the ethical estimation of action. Whether we are reviewing the actions of ourselves or of others, what we seem to do, in the first instance, is to refer them to some class, or associate them with certain actions of a similar kind which are familiar to us, and, then, when their character has thus been determined, they excite the appropriate feeling of approbation or disapprobation, praise or censure. Thus, as soon as we have realised that a statement is a lie or an act is fraudulent, we at once experience a feeling of indignation or disgust at the person who has made the statement or committed the act. And, in the same way, as soon as we have recognised that an act is brave or generous, we regard with esteem or admiration the doer of it. But, though the feeling of approbation or disapprobation follows instantaneously on the act of judgment, the recognition of the character of the action, or its reference to a class, which constitutes this act of judgment, may be, and often is, a process of considerable length and complexity. Take the case of a lie. What did the man really say? In what sense did he employ the words used? What was the extent of his knowledge at the time that he made the statement? And what was his intention? These and possibly other questions have to be answered, before we are justified in accusing him of having told a lie. When the offence is not only a moral but a legal one, the act of determining the character of the action in question is often the result of a prolonged enquiry, extending over weeks or months. No sooner, however, is the intellectual process completed, and the action duly labelled as a lie, or a theft, or a fraud, or an act of cruelty or ingratitude, or the like, than the appropriate ethical emotion is at once excited. The intellectual process may also be exceedingly rapid, or even instantaneous, and always is so when we have no doubt as to the nature either of the action or of the intention or of the motives, but its characteristic, as distinguished from the ethical emotion, is that it may take time, and, except in perfectly clear cases or on very sudden emergencies requiring subsequent action, always ought to do so.

We are now in a position to see the source of much confusion in the ordinary mode of speaking and writing on the subject of the moral faculty, the moral judgment, the moral feeling, the moral sense, the conscience, and kindred terms. The instantaneous, and the apparently instinctive, authoritative, and absolute character of the act of moral approbation or disapprobation attaches to the emotional, and not to the intellectual part of the process. When an action has once been pronounced to be right or wrong, morally good or evil, or has been referred to some well-known class of actions whose ethical character is already determined, the emotion of approval or disapproval is excited and follows as a matter of course. There is no reasoning or hesitation about it, simply because the act is not a reasoning act. Hence, it appears to be instinctive, and becomes invested with those superior attributes of authoritativeness, absoluteness, and even infallibility, which are not unnaturally ascribed to an act in which, there being no process of reasoning, there seems to be no room for error. And, indeed, the feelings of moral approbation and disapprobation can never be properly described as erroneous, though they are frequently misapplied. The error attaches to the preliminary process of reasoning, reference, or classification, and, if this be wrongly conducted, there is no justification for the feeling which is consequent upon it. But, instead of our asking for the justification of the feeling in the rational process which has preceded it, we often unconsciously justify our reasoning by the feeling, and thus the whole process assumes the unreflective character which properly belongs only to the emotional part of it. It is the want of a clear distinction between the logical process which determines the character of an act,--the moral judgment,--and the emotion which immediately supervenes when the character of the act is determined,--the moral feeling,--that accounts for the exaggerated epithets which are often attributed to the operations of the moral faculty, and for the haste and negligence in which men are consequently encouraged to indulge, when arriving at their moral decisions. Let it be recollected that, when we have time for reflexion, we cannot take too much pains in forming our decisions upon conduct, for there is always a possibility of error in our judgments, but that, when our judgments are formed, we ought to give free scope to the emotions which they naturally evoke, and then we shall develop a conscience, so to speak, at once enlightened and sensitive, we shall combine accuracy and justness of judgment with delicacy and strength of feeling.

There remains the question whether the feelings of approval and disapproval, which supervene on our moral judgments, admit of any explanation, or whether they are to be regarded as ultimate facts of our mental constitution. It seems to me that, on a little reflexion, we are led to adopt the former alternative. What are the classes of acts, under their most general aspect, which elicit the feelings of moral approbation and disapprobation? They are such as promote, or tend to promote, the good either of ourselves or of others. Now the feelings of which these classes of acts are the direct object are respectively the self-regarding and the sympathetic feelings, or, as they have been somewhat uncouthly called, the egoistic and altruistic feelings. We have a variety of appetites and desires, which centre in ourselves, including what has been called rational self-love, or a desire for what, on cool reflexion, we conceive to be our own highest good on the whole, as well as self-respect, or a regard for our own dignity and character, and for our own opinion of ourselves. When any of these various appetites or desires are gratified, we feel satisfaction, and, on the other hand, when they are thwarted, we feel dissatisfaction. Similarly, we have a number of affections, of which others are the object, some of them of a malevolent or resentful, but most of them of a benevolent character, including a general desire to confer all the happiness that we can. Here, again, we feel satisfaction, when our affections are gratified, and dissatisfaction, when they are thwarted. Now these feelings of satisfaction and dissatisfaction, which are called reflex feelings, because they are reflected, as it were, from the objects of our desires, include, though they are by no means coextensive with, the feelings of moral approbation and disapprobation. When, for instance, we gratify the appetites of hunger or thirst, or our love of curiosity or power, we feel satisfaction, but we can hardly be said to regard the gratification of these appetites or feelings with moral approval or disapproval. We perform thousands of acts, and see thousands of acts performed, every day, which never excite any moral feeling whatever. But there are few men in whom an undoubted act of kindness or generosity or resistance to temptation would not at once elicit admiration or respect, or, if they reflected on such acts in their own case, of self-approval. Now, what are the circumstances which distinguish these acts which merely cause us satisfaction from those which elicit the moral feeling of approbation? This question is one by no means easy to answer, and the solution of it must obviously depend to some extent on the moral surroundings and prepossessions of the person who undertakes to answer it. But, attempting to take as wide a survey as possible of those acts which, in different persons, elicit moral approbation or disapprobation, I will endeavour to discriminate the characteristics which they have in common.

All those acts, then, it seems to me, which elicit a distinctively moral feeling have been the result of some conflict amongst the various desires and affections, or, to adopt the more ordinary phraseology, of a conflict of motives. We neither approve nor disapprove of acts with regard to which there seems to have been little or no choice, which appear to have resulted naturally from the pre-existing circumstances. Thus, if a well-to-do man pays his debts promptly, or a man of known poverty asks to have the time of payment deferred, we neither visit the one with praise nor the other with censure, though, if their conduct were reversed, we should censure the former and praise the latter. The reason of this difference of treatment is plain. There is not, or at least need not be, any conflict, in the case of the well-to-do man, between his own convenience or any reasonable gratification of his desires and the satisfaction of a just claim. Hence, in paying the debt promptly, he is only acting as we might expect him to act, and his conduct excites no moral feeling on our part, though, if he were to act differently, he would incur our censure. The poor man, on the other hand, must have put himself to some inconvenience and exercised some self-denial in order to meet his engagement at the exact time at which the payment became due, and hence he merits our praise, though, if he had acted otherwise, the circumstances might have excused him.

Another characteristic of acts which we praise or blame, in the case of others, or approve or disapprove, on reflexion, in our own case, seems to be that they must possess some importance. The great majority of our acts are too trivial to merit any notice, such as is implied in a moral judgment. When a man makes way for another in the street, or refrains from eating or drinking more than is good for him, neither he nor the bystander probably ever thinks of regarding the act as a meritorious one. It is taken as a matter of course, though the opposite conduct might, under certain circumstances, be of sufficient importance to incur censure. It is impossible here, as in most other cases where we speak of 'importance,' to draw a definite line, but it may at least be laid down that an act, in order to be regarded as moral or immoral, must be of sufficient importance to arrest attention, and stimulate reflexion.

Thus far, then, we have arrived at the conclusion that acts which are the objects of moral approbation and disapprobation must have a certain importance, and must be the result of a certain amount of conflict between different motives. But we have not as yet attempted to detect any principle of discrimination between those acts which are the objects of praise or approbation and those which are the objects of censure or disapprobation. Now it seems to me that such a principle may be found in the fact that all those acts of others which we praise or those acts of ourselves which, on reflexion, we approve involve some amount of sacrifice, whereas all those acts of others which we blame, or those acts of ourselves which, on reflexion, we disapprove involve some amount of self-indulgence. The conflict is between a man's own lower and higher good, or between his own good and the greater good of others, or, in certain cases, as we shall see presently, between the lesser good of some, reinforced by considerations of self-interest or partiality, and the greater good of others, not so reinforced, or even, occasionally, between the pleasure or advantage of others and a disproportionate injury to himself; and he who, in the struggle, gives the preference to the former of these motives usually becomes the object of censure or, on reflexion, of self-disapprobation, while he who gives the preference to the latter becomes the object of praise or, on reflexion, of self-approbation. I shall endeavour to illustrate this position by a few instances mostly taken from common life. We praise a man who, by due economy, makes decent provision for himself in old age, as we blame a man who fails to do so. Quite apart from any public or social considerations, we admire and applaud in the one man the power of self-restraint and the habit of foresight, which enable him to subordinate his immediate gratifications to his larger interests in the remote future, and to forego sensual and passing pleasures for the purpose of preserving his self-respect and personal independence in later life. And we admire and applaud him still more, if to these purely self-regarding considerations he adds the social one of wishing to avoid becoming a burden on his family or his friends or the public. Just in the same way, we condemn the other man, who, rather than sacrifice his immediate gratification, will incur the risk of forfeiting his self-respect and independence in after years as well as of making others suffer for his improvidence. A man who, by the exercise of similar economy and forethought, makes provision for his family or relations we esteem still more than the man who simply makes provision for himself, because the sacrifice of passing pleasures is generally still greater, and because there is also, in this case, a total sacrifice of all self-regarding interests, except, perhaps, self-respect and reputation, for the sake of others. Similarly, the man who has a family or relations dependent upon him, and who neglects to make future provision for them, deservedly incurs our censure far more than the man who merely neglects to make provision for himself, because his self-indulgence has to contend against the full force of the social as well as the higher self-regarding motives, and its persistence is, therefore, the less excusable.

I will next take the familiar case of a trust, voluntarily undertaken, but involving considerable trouble to the trustee, a case of a much more complicated character than the last. If the trustee altogether neglects or does not devote a reasonable amount of attention to the affairs of the trust, there is no doubt that, besides any legal penalties which he may incur, he merits moral censure. Rather than sacrifice his own ease or his own interests, he violates the obligation which he has undertaken and brings inconvenience, or possibly disaster, to those whose interests he has bound himself to protect. But the demands of the trust may become so excessive as to tax the time and pains of the trustee to a far greater extent than could ever have been anticipated, and to interfere seriously with his other employments. In this case no reasonable person, I presume, would censure the trustee for endeavouring, even at some inconvenience or expense to the persons for whose benefit the trust existed, to release himself from his obligation or to devolve part of the work on a professional adviser. While, however, the work connected with the trust did not interfere with other obligations or with the promotion of the welfare of others, no one, I imagine, would censure the trustee for continuing to perform it, to his own inconvenience or disadvantage, if he chose to do so. His neighbours might, perhaps, say that he was foolish, but they would hardly go to the length of saying that he acted wrongly. Neither, on the other hand, would they be likely to praise him, as the sacrifice he was undergoing would be out of proportion to the good attained by it, and the interests of others to which he was postponing his own interests would not be so distinctly greater as to warrant the act of self-effacement. But now let us suppose that, in attending to the interests of the trust, he is neglecting the interests of others who have a claim upon him, or impairing his own efficiency as a public servant or a professional man. If the interests thus at stake were plainly much greater than those of the trust, as they might well be, the attitude of neutrality would soon be converted into one of positive censure, unless he took means to extricate himself from the difficulty in which he was placed.

The supposition just made illustrates the fact that the moral feelings may attach themselves not only to cases in which the collision is between a man's own higher and lower good, or between his own good and that of another, but also to those in which the competition is entirely between the good of others. It may be worth while to illustrate this last class of cases by one or two additional examples. A man tells a lie in order to screen a friend. The act is a purely social one, for he stands in no fear of his friend, and expects no return. It might be said that the competition, in this example, is between serving his friend and wounding his own self-respect. But the consciousness of cowardice and meanness which attends a lie spoken in a man's own interest hardly attaches to a lie spoken for the purpose of protecting another. And, any way, a little reflexion might show that the apparently benevolent intention comes into collision with a very extensive and very stringent social obligation, that of not impairing our confidence in one another's assertions. Without maintaining that there are no conceivable circumstances under which a man would be justified in committing a breach of veracity, it may at least be said that, in the lives of most men, there is not likely to occur any case in which the greater social good would not be attained by the observation of the general rule to tell the truth rather than by the recognition of an exception in favour of a lie, even though that lie were told for purely benevolent reasons. In all those circumstances in which there is a keen sense of comradeship, as at school or college, or in the army or navy, this is a principle which requires to be constantly kept in view, and to be constantly enforced. The not infrequent breach of it, under such circumstances, affords a striking illustration of the manner in which the laws of honour, spoken of in the first chapter, occasionally over-ride the wider social sentiment and even the dictates of personal morality, ***Esprit de corps*** is, doubtless, a noble sentiment, and, on the whole, productive of much good, but, when it comes into collision with the more general rules of morality, its effects are simply pernicious. I will next take an example of the conflict between two impulses, each having for its object the good of others, from the very familiar case of a man having to appoint to, or vote in the election to, a vacant office or situation. The interests of the public service or of some institution require that the most competent candidate should be preferred. But a relative, or a friend, or a political ally is standing. Affection, therefore, or friendship, or loyalty to party ties often dictates one course of conduct, and regard for the public interests another. When the case is thus plainly stated, there are probably few men who would seriously maintain that we ought to subordinate the wider to the narrower considerations, and still, in practice, there are few men who have the courage to act constantly on what is surely the right principle in this matter, and, what is worse still, even if they did, they would not always be sustained by public opinion, while they would be almost certain to be condemned by the circle in which they move. So frequently do the difficulties of this position recur, that I have often heard a shrewd friend observe that no man who was fit for the exercise of patronage would ever desire to be entrusted with it. The moral rule in ordinary cases is plain enough; it is to appoint or vote for the candidate who is most competent to fulfil the duties of the post to be filled up. There are exceptional cases in which it may be allowable slightly to modify this rule, as where it is desirable to encourage particular services, or particular nationalities, or the like, but, even in these cases, the rule of superior competency ought to be the preponderating consideration. Parliamentary and, in a lesser degree, municipal elections, of course, form a class apart. Here, in the selection of candidates within the party, superior competency ought to be the guiding consideration, but, in the election itself, the main object being to promote or prevent the passing of certain public measures, the elector quite rightly votes for those who will give effect to his opinions, irrespectively of personal qualifications, though, even in these cases, there might be an amount of unfitness which would warrant neutrality or opposition. Peculiarly perplexing cases of competition between the rival claims of others sometimes occur in the domain of the resentful feelings, which, in their purified and rationalised form, constitute the sense of justice. My servant, or a friend, or a relative, has committed a theft. Shall I prosecute him? A general regard to the public welfare undoubtedly demands that I should do so. There are few obligations more imperative on the individual citizen than that of denouncing and prosecuting crime. But, in the present case, there is the personal tie, involving the obligation of protection and assistance. This tie, obviously, must count for something, as a rival consideration. No man, except under the most extreme circumstances, would prosecute his wife, or his father, or his mother. The question, then, is how far this consideration is to count against the other, and much must, evidently, depend on the degree of relationship or of previous intimacy, the time and amount and kind of service, and the like. A similar conflict of motives arises when the punishment invoked would entail the culprit's ruin, or that of his wife or family or others who are dependent upon him. It is impossible, in cases of this kind, to lay down beforehand any strict rules of conduct, and the rectitude of the decision must largely turn on the experience, skill, and honesty of the person who attempts to resolve the difficulty.

Instances of the last division, where the conflict is between the pleasure or advantage of others and a disproportionate injury to oneself, are of comparatively infrequent occurrence. It is not often that a man hesitates sufficiently between his own manifest disadvantage and the small gains or pleasures of his neighbours to make this class of cases of much importance to the moralist. As a rule, we may be trusted to take care of ourselves, and other people credit us sufficiently with this capacity not to trade very much upon the weakness of mere good-nature, however much they may trade upon our ignorance and folly. The most familiar example, perhaps, of acts of imprudence of the kind here contemplated is to be found in the facility with which some people yield to social temptations, as where they drink too much, or bet, or play cards, when they know that they will most likely lose their money, out of a feeling of mere good fellowship; or where, from the mere desire to amuse others, they give parties which are beyond their means. The gravest example is to be found in certain cases of seduction. Instances of men making large and imprudent sacrifices of money for inadequate objects are very rare, and are rather designated as foolish than wrong. With regard to all the failings and offences which fall under this head, it may be remarked that, from their false show of generosity, society is apt to treat them too venially, except where they entail degradation or disgrace. If it be asked how actions of this kind, seeing that they are done out of some regard to others, can be described as involving self-indulgence, or the resistance to them can be looked on in the light of sacrifice, it may be replied that the conflict is between a feeling of sociality or a spirit of over-complaisance or the like, on the one side, and a man's self-respect or a regard to his own highest interests, on the other, and that some natures find it much easier to yield to the former than to maintain the latter. It is quite possible that the spirit of sacrifice may be exhibited in the maintenance, against temptation, of a man's own higher interests, and the spirit of self-indulgence in weakly yielding to a perverted sympathy or an exaggerated regard for the opinions of others.

Before concluding this chapter, there are a few objections to be met and explanations to be made. In the first place, it may be objected that the theory I have adopted, that the moral feeling is excited only where there has been a conflict of motives, runs counter to the ordinary view, that acts proceeding from a virtuous or vicious habit are done without any struggle and almost without any consciousness of their import. I do not at all deny that a habit may become so perfect that the acts proceeding from it cease to involve any struggle between conflicting motives, but, in this case, I conceive that our approbation or disapprobation is transferred from the individual acts to the habit from which they spring, and that what we really applaud or condemn is the character rather than the actions, or at least the actions simply as indicative of the character. And the reason that we often praise or blame acts proceeding from habit more than acts proceeding from momentary impulse is that we associate such acts with a good or evil character, as the case may be, and, therefore, include the character as well as the acts in the judgment which we pass upon them.

It may possibly have occurred to the reader that, in the latter part of this chapter, I have been somewhat inconsistent in referring usually to the social sanction of praise and blame rather than to the distinctively moral sanction of self-approbation and self-disapprobation. I have employed this language solely for the sake of convenience, and to avoid the cumbrous phraseology which the employment of the other phrases would sometimes have occasioned. In a civilized and educated community, the social sentiment may, on almost all points except those which involve obscure or delicate considerations of morality, be taken to be identical with the moral sentiment of the most reflective members of the society, and hence in the tolerably obvious instances which I have selected there was no need to draw any distinction between the two, and I have felt myself at liberty to be guided purely by considerations of convenience. All that I have said of the praise or blame, the applause or censure, of others, of course, admits of being transferred to the feelings with which, on reflexion, we regard our own acts.

I am aware that the expressions, 'higher and lower good,' 'greater and lesser good,' are more or less vague. But the traditional acceptation of the terms sufficiently fixes their meaning to enable them to serve as a guide to moral conduct and moral feeling, especially when modified by the experience and reflexion of men who have given habitual attention to the working of their own motives and the results of their own practice. As I shall shew in the next chapter, any terms which we employ to designate the test of moral action and the objects of the moral feeling are indefinite, and must depend, to some extent, on the subjective interpretation of the individual. All that we can do is to avail ourselves of the most adequate and intelligible terms that we can find. But, admitting the necessary indefiniteness of the terms, it may be asked whether it can really be meant, as a general proposition, that the praise of others and our approbation of ourselves, on reflexion, attach to acts in which we subordinate our own good to the greater good of others, however slight the preponderance of our neighbour's good over out own may be. If we have to undergo an almost equal risk in order to save another, or, in order to promote another's interests, to forego interests almost as great, is not our conduct more properly designated as weak or quixotic, than noble or generous? This would not, I think, be the answer of mankind at large to the question, or that of any person whose moral sentiments had been developed under healthy influences. When a man, at the risk of his own life, saves another from drowning, or, at a similar risk, protects his comrade in battle, or, rushing into the midst of a fire, attempts to rescue the helpless victims, surely the feeling of the bystanders is that of admiration, and not of pity or contempt. When a man, with his life in his hands, goes forth on a missionary or a philanthropic enterprise, like Xavier, or Henry Martyn, or Howard, or Livingstone, or Patteson, or when a man, like Frederick Vyner, insists on transferring his own chance of escape from a murderous gang of brigands to his married friend, humanity at large rightly regards itself as his debtor, and ordinary men feel that their very nature has been ennobled and exalted by his example. But it is not only these acts of widely recognised heroism that exact a response from mankind. In many a domestic circle, there are men and women, who habitually sacrifice their own ease and comfort to the needs of an aged or sick or helpless relative, and, surely, it is not with scorn for their weakness that their neighbours, who know their privations, regard them, but with sympathy and respect for their patience and self-denial. The pecuniary risks and sacrifices which men are ready to make for one another, in the shape of sureties and bonds and loans and gifts, are familiar to us all, and, though these are often unscrupulously wrung from a thoughtless or over-pliant good-nature, yet there are many instances in which men knowingly, deliberately, and at considerable danger or loss to themselves, postpone their own security or convenience to the protection or relief of their friends. It is in cases of this kind, perhaps, that the line between weakness and generosity is most difficult to draw, and, where a man has others dependent on him for assistance or support, the weakness which yields to the solicitations of a reckless or unscrupulous friend may become positively culpable.

The last class of instances will be sufficient to shew that it is not always easy to determine where the good of others is greater than our own. Nor is it ever possible to determine this question with mathematical exactness. Men may, therefore, be at least excused if, before sacrificing their own interests or pleasures, they require that the good of others for which they make the sacrifice shall be plainly preponderant. And, even then, there is a wide margin between the acts which we praise for their heroism, or generosity, or self-denial, and those which we condemn for their baseness, or meanness, or selfishness. It must never be forgotten, in the treatment of questions of morality, that there is a large number of acts which we neither praise nor blame, and this is emphatically the case where the competition is between a man's own interests and those of his neighbours. We applaud generosity; we censure meanness: but there is a large intermediate class of acts which can neither be designated as generous nor mean. It will be observed that, in my enumeration of the classes of acts to which praise and blame, self-approbation and self-disapprobation attach, I have carefully drawn a distinction between the invariable connexion which obtains between certain acts and the ethical approval of ourselves or others, and the only general connexion which obtains between the omission of those acts and the ethical feeling of disapproval. Simply to fall short of the ethical standard which we approve neither merits nor receives censure, though there is a degree of deficiency, determined roughly by society at large and by each individual for himself, at which this indifference is converted into positive condemnation. A like neutral zone of acts which we neither applaud nor condemn, of course, exists also in the case of acts which simply affect ourselves or simply affect others, though it does not seem to be so extensive as in the case where the conflict of motives is between the interests of others and those of ourselves.

In determining the cases in which we shall subordinate our own interests to those of others, or do good to others at our own risk or loss, it is essential that we should take account of the remote as well as the immediate effects of actions; and, moreover, that we should enquire into their general tendencies, or, in other words, ask ourselves what would happen if everybody or many people acted as we propose to act. Thus, at first sight, it might seem as if a rich man, at a comparatively small sacrifice to himself, might promote the greater good of his poor neighbours by distributing amongst them what to them would be considerable sums of money. If I have ten thousand a year, why should I not make fifty poor families happy by endowing them with a hundred a year each, which to them would be a handsome competency? The loss of five thousand a year would be to me simply an abridgment of superfluous luxuries, which I could soon learn to dispense with, while to them the gain of a hundred a year would be the substitution of comfort for penury and of case for perpetual struggle. The answer is that, in the first place, I should probably not, in the long run, be making these families really happy. The change of circumstances would, undoubtedly, confer considerable pleasure, while it continued to be a novelty, but their improved circumstances, when they became accustomed to them, would soon be out-balanced by the ***ennui*** produced by want of employment; while, the motive to exertion being removed, and the taste for luxuries stimulated, they or the next generation would probably lapse again into poverty, which would be all the more keenly felt for their temporary enjoyment of prosperity. Moreover, I should be injuring the community at large, by withdrawing a number of persons from industrial employments and transferring them to the non-productive classes.

Again, if the five thousand a year were withdrawn not from my personal expenditure, but from industrial enterprises in which I was engaged, I should be actually depriving the families of many workmen and artisans of the fruits of their honest labour for the purpose of enabling a smaller number of families to live in sloth and indolence. But, now, suppose the case I have imagined to become a general one, and that it was a common occurrence for rich men to dispense their superfluous wealth amongst their poorer neighbours, without demanding any return in labour or services. The result would inevitably be the creation of a large class of idle persons, who would probably soon become a torment to themselves, while their descendants, often brought up to no employment and with an insufficient income to support them, would probably lapse into pauperism. The effect on the community at large, if the evil became widely spread, would be the paralysis of trade and commerce. Of course, I am aware that these evils would be, to a certain extent, modified in practice by the good sense of the recipients, some of whom might employ their money on reproductive industries instead of on merely furnishing themselves with the means of living at their ease; but that the general tendency would be that which I have intimated no one, I think, who is acquainted with the indolent propensities of human nature, can well doubt. Similar results might be shewn to follow from an indiscriminate distribution of charity on a smaller scale. It seems hard-hearted to refuse a shilling to a beggar, or a guinea to a charitable association, when one would hardly miss the sum at the end of the week or the month. But, if we could trace all the consequences, direct and remote, of these apparent acts of benevolence, we should often see that the small act of sacrifice on our own part was by no means efficacious in promoting the 'greater good' of the recipient, and still less of society at large. A life of vagrancy or indolence may easily be made more attractive than one of honest industry, and well-meant efforts to anticipate all the wants and misfortunes of the poor may often have the effect of making them careless of the future and of destroying all elements of independence and providence in their character. Another instance of the contrast between the immediate and remote, or apparent and real, results of acts of intended beneficence is to be found in the prodigality with which well-to-do persons often distribute gratuities amongst servants. These gratuities have the immediate effect of giving gratification to the recipients and securing better service to the donors, but they have often the remote and more permanent effect of rendering the recipients servile and corrupt, and (as in the case of railway porters) of depriving poorer or less prodigal persons of services to which they are equally entitled.

In adducing these illustrations, I must not be understood to be advocating or defending a selfish employment of superfluous wealth, but to be shewing the evils which may result from an unenlightened benevolence, and the importance of ascertaining that the 'greater good of others,' to which we sacrifice our own interests or enjoyments, is a real, and not merely an apparent good, and, moreover, that our conduct, if it became general, would promote the welfare of the community at large, and not merely particular sections of it to the injury of the rest.

To sum up the results of this chapter, we may repeat that we must distinguish carefully between the intellectual act of moral judgment, or the judgment we pass on matters of conduct, and the emotional act of moral feeling, or the feeling which supervenes upon that judgment, and that, so far as we can give a precise definition of the latter, it is an indirect or reflex form of one or other of the sympathetic, resentful, or self-regarding feelings, occurring when, on consideration, we realise that, in matters involving a conflict of motives and of sufficient importance to arrest our attention and stimulate our reflexion, one or other of these feelings has been gratified or thwarted: moreover, that we praise, in the case of others, and approve, in our own case, all those actions of the above kind, in which a man subordinates his own lower to his higher good, or his own good to the greater good of others, or, when the interests only of others are at stake, the lesser good of some to the greater good of others, as well as, under certain circumstances, those actions in which he refuses to subordinate his own greater good to the lesser good of others; while we blame, in the case of others, and disapprove, in our own case, all those actions of the above kind, in which he manifestly and distinctly (for there is a large neutral zone of actions, which we neither applaud nor condemn) subordinates his own higher to his lower good, or the greater good of others to his own lesser good, or, where the interests only of others are at stake, the greater good of some to the lesser good of others, or, lastly, under certain circumstances, the lesser good of others to the greater good of himself, especially where that greater good is the good of his higher nature.

Even at the present stage of our enquiry, it must be tolerably evident to the reader that moral progress, if such a fact exist, will be due mainly to the increasing accuracy and the extended applications of our moral judgments, or, in other words, to the development of the rational rather than the emotional element in the ethical act. The moral feeling follows on the moral judgment, and awards praise or blame, experiences satisfaction or dissatisfaction, in accordance with the intellectual decisions which have preceded it. The character of the feeling, therefore, as distinct from its intensity, is already determined for it by a previous process. And its intensity is undoubtedly greater amongst primitive and uneducated men than it is in civilized life. Amongst ourselves, not only are the feelings of approbation and disapprobation themselves largely modified by the account we take of mixed motives, qualifying circumstances, and the like, but the expression of, them is still further restrained by the caution which the civilized man habitually practises in the presence of others. Indeed, great, in many respects, as are the advantages of this moderation and restraint, there is a certain danger that, as civilisation advances, the approval of virtue and the disapproval of vice may cease to be expressed in sufficiently plain and emphatic terms. But, on the other hand, with the extension of experience and the ever-improving discipline of the intellectual faculties, the moral judgment, we may already presume (for the confirmation of this presumption I must refer to the next chapter), will always be growing in accuracy, receiving further applications, and becoming a more and more adequate representative of facts. The analysis, therefore, of the moral act, with which we have been mainly engaged in the foregoing chapter, besides being essential to the determination of any theoretical problem of ethics, has a most important practical bearing from the indication which it affords of the direction in which moral progress is, in the future, most likely to be found.

It must never be forgotten, however, that men may know what is right and do what is wrong, and, hence, the due stimulation of the moral emotions, so that they may respond to the improved moral judgments, is at once an indispensable branch of moral education and an indispensable condition of moral progress. But this is the function, not so much of the scientific moralist, as of the parent, the instructor of youth, the poet, the dramatist, the novelist, the journalist, the artist, and, above all, of the religious teacher.

CHAPTER IV.
THE MORAL TEST AND ITS JUSTIFICATION.

The moral feeling, as we have seen, follows immediately and necessarily on the moral judgment. But what considerations guide the moral judgment? Our moral judgments, as we have also seen, are the result of a logical process of reference to a class or of association with similars. This particular action is like certain other actions, or belongs to a class of actions, which we habitually regard as right or wrong, and, consequently, as soon as the reference or association is made, the moral feeling supervenes. Now, in this process, there are two possible sources of error. In the first place, the act of reference or association may be faulty, and the action may not really belong to the class to which we refer or really be like the other actions with which we associate it. This fault is one of classification, and can only be remedied, as all other faulty acts of classification, by learning to discriminate between the essential and the non-essential marks of similarity, and insisting on the presence of the essential marks. In criminal cases, this is one of the functions of the jury, and, unless they exercise great care, they may easily be mistaken as to whether an alleged act of fraud, theft, assault, &c., was really an act of that kind. But, even if the action be referred to its right head, there remains the second question whether we are really justified in regarding the class of actions itself as right or wrong. Failure to prosecute for or punish heresy or witchcraft was at one time regarded at least as wrong as failure to punish or prosecute for theft or murder would now be. To decline to fight a duel was, till quite recently, to place yourself outside the pale of gentlemen. A reluctance to sacrifice herself on the funeral pile of her dead husband was, till the practice of Suttee was abolished by the British government, one of the most immoral traits which a Brahman widow could exhibit. Now, have we any means of discriminating, and, if so, how do we discriminate, between those acts which are really, and those which are only reputed, right or wrong? That there is great need of such a test, if it can be discovered, is plain. The wide divergences of opinion on matters of conduct in different ages, in different countries, in different classes of society, and even amongst men of the same class In the same country and at the same time, shew at once the vast importance of ascertaining some common measure of actions, and that there is no uniform rule of right and wrong to be found in the human mind itself. If there is such a rule, it must be derived from some external considerations, and, if there is no such rule, then morality must be, to a large extent, a matter of prejudice, fancy, and caprice. Now I conceive that there is a simple mode of ascertaining whether there is any test of actions other than the merely subjective determinations of our own minds, or, in other words, whether there are any reasons or external considerations by which the mind guides itself in its decisions on matters of conduct. Do our moral opinions merely vary, or do they grow? Is there any progress to be traced in morality, or does it simply oscillate, within certain limits, round a fixed point? If some 'simple' and 'innate' idea of right, or some universal sense, were the test of morality, then we might expect that the moral decisions of all men would be uniform, or, at least, approximately uniform; if, on the other hand, there were no test at all, or, what amounts to much the same thing, a merely personal test, then we might expect that the moral judgments of mankind would vary arbitrarily according to the disposition and temperament of each individual man. But, if there be a test derived from external considerations and capable of being applied to particular cases by the ordinary processes of reasoning, then we may fairly expect that, as the opportunities of observation and experience increase, the test will be applied more widely and more accurately, and that the science of conduct will grow, like all other sciences, with the advance of knowledge and of general civilisation. Now, what, as a matter of fact, has been the case? Can anyone affect to doubt that the morality of civilized countries is far higher and purer, and far better adapted to secure the preservation and progress of society, than the customs of savage or barbaric tribes? Or, however enamoured a man may be of classical antiquity, is there any one who would be prepared to change the ethical code and the prevailing ethical sentiment of modern times for those of the Greeks or Romans? Or, again, should we be willing, in this respect, to go back three hundred, or two hundred, or even one hundred years in our own history? Are not the abolition of slavery, the improved and improving treatment of captives taken in war, of women and children, of the distressed and unfortunate, and even of the lower animals, alone sufficient to mark the difference between the morality of earlier and of later times? I shall assume, then, that there is a test of conduct, and that this test is of such a character that its continued application, by individual thinkers or by mankind at large, consciously or semi-consciously, is sufficient to account for the existence of a progressive morality. But, if so, it must be a test which experience enables us to apply with increasing accuracy, and which is derived from external considerations, or, in other words, from the observation of the effects and tendencies of actions. And here I may observe, parenthetically, that to make 'conscience' or 'moral reason' or 'moral sense' the test of action, as, for instance, Bishop Butler appears to do in the case of conscience, is, even on the supposition of the independent existence of these so-called 'faculties,' to confound the judge with the law which governs his decisions, the 'faculty' with the rules in accordance with which it operates. Limiting ourselves, therefore, to a test which is derived from a consideration of the results, direct and indirect, immediate and remote, of our actions, we simply have to enquire what is the characteristic in these results which men have in view when they try to act rightly, and which they mistake, ignore, or lose sight of, when they act wrongly.

There are, in the main, three answers to this question, though they are rather different modes, I conceive, of presenting the same idea, than distinct and independent explanations. It may be said that we look to the manner in which the action will affect the happiness or pleasure of those whom it concerns, or their welfare or well-being, or the development or perfection of their character. Now it seems to me that these are by no means necessarily antagonistic modes of speaking, and that, in attempting to determine the test of right action, they are all useful as complementing each other. There is, however, a view of the measure of actions which, though derived from external considerations, is opposed to them all, and which it may be desirable to notice at once, with the object of eliminating it from our enquiry. It is that we are only concerned with actions so far as they affect ourselves, and that, providing we observe the law of the land, which will punish us if we do not observe it, we are under no further obligations to our fellow-citizens. This paradox, for such it is, has mainly acquired notoriety though the advocacy of Hobbes, though it has sometimes been ignorantly attributed to Bentham and other writers of what is called the utilitarian school. But, be this as it may, it is so plainly inconsistent with some of the most obvious facts of human nature, and specially with the existence of that large and essential group of emotions which we call the sympathetic feelings, as well as with the constitution of family, social, and civic life, that it is unnecessary here further to discuss it. The views now generally accepted as to the origin of society in the family or tribal relations are alike irreconcileable with the selfish psychology from which Hobbes educes his system of morality and with that 'state of nature in which every man was at war with every man' from which he traces the growth of law and government. Reverting, therefore, to those tests of conduct which recognise, the independent existence of social as well as self-regarding springs of action, I shall now make some remarks on the appropriateness and adequacy, for the purpose of designating such tests, of the three classes of terms, noticed above. To begin with happiness or pleasure. Taking happiness to mean the balance of pleasures over pains, and degrees of happiness the proportions of this balance, it will be sufficient if I confine myself to the word 'pleasure.' One statement, then, of the test of the morality or rightness of an action is that it should result in a larger amount of pleasure than pain to all those whom it affects. But it is at once objected that there is the greatest variety of pleasures and pains, intellectual, moral, aesthetic, sympathetic, sensual, and so on; and it is asked how are we to determine their respective values, and to strike the balance between the conflicting kinds? How much sensual pleasure would compensate for the pangs of an evil conscience, or what amount of intellectual enjoyment would allay the cravings of hunger or thirst? The only escape from this difficulty is frankly to acknowledge that there are some pleasures and pains which are incommensurable with one other, and that, therefore, where they are concerned, we must forego the attempt at comparison, and so act as to compass the immeasurably greater pleasure or avoid the immeasurably greater pain. Especially is this the case with the pleasures and pains attendant on the exercise of the moral feelings. A man who is tormented with the recollection of having committed a great crime will, as the phrase goes, 'take pleasure in nothing;' while, similarly, a man who is enjoying the retrospect of having done his duty, in some important crisis, will care little for obloquy or even for the infliction of physical suffering. Making this admission, then, as well as recognising the fact that our pleasures differ in quality as well as in volume, so that the pleasures of the higher part of our nature, the religious, the intellectual, the moral, the aesthetic, the sympathetic nature, affect us with a different kind of enjoyment from the sensual pleasures, or those which are derived from them, we may rightly regard the tendency to produce a balance of pleasure over pain as the test of the goodness of an action, and the effort and intention to perform acts having this tendency as the test of the morality of the agent. But when we enunciate the production of pleasure as our aim, or the balance of pleasure-producing over pain-producing results as the test of right action, we are not always understood to have admitted these explanations, and, consequently, there is always a danger of our being supposed to degrade morality by identifying it with the gratification, in ourselves and others, of the coarser and more material impulses of our nature. Though, then, if due distinctions and admissions be made, the tendency to produce, in the long run, the greatest amount of happiness or misery, pleasure or pain, may be taken as the test of the goodness or badness of an action, the phraseology is so misleading, and so liable to frustrate the practical objects of the moralist, that it is desirable, if possible, to find terms not equally lending themselves to misinterpretation and perversion. Let us now, then, consider whether we are supplied with such terms in the phrases 'perfection' or 'development' of 'character.' It is a noble idea of human action to suppose that its end is the perfection of individual men, or the development of their various capacities to the utmost extent that is available. And yet, as the phrases 'pleasure' and 'happiness' are apt too exclusively to suggest material well-being and the gratification of the more animal parts of our nature, so the phrases 'perfection' or 'development' of 'character' are apt altogether to keep out of sight these necessary pre-suppositions of a healthy and progressive condition of humanity. Unless there were some standard of comfortable living, and a constant effort not only to maintain but to improve it, and unless some zest were given to every-day life by the gratification of the appetites, within reasonable limits, and the endeavour to obtain the means of indulging them, men, constituted as they are, would be in danger of sinking into sloth, squalor, and indigence, and, to the great mass of mankind, the opportunity of developing and perfecting their higher nature would never occur. We seem, therefore, to require some term which will not only suggest the highest results of moral endeavour, but also the conditions which, in the case of humanity, are essential to the attainment of those results. Moreover, to a greater extent even than the words 'pleasure' and 'happiness,' the expressions 'perfection' and 'development' of 'character' are in danger of being supposed to imply an exclusive reference to self. It is true that we cannot properly develope our characters, much less attain to all the perfection of which they are capable, without quickening the moral feeling and giving larger scope to the sympathetic emotions; but, in the mere attempt to improve their own nature, men are very apt to lose sight of their relations to others. The phrases ought, however, to be taken, and usually are intended to be taken, to include the effort to improve the character of others as well as our own; and if this extension of their meaning be well understood, and it is also understood that the development or perfection of character implies certain conditions of material comfort and the gratification, within reasonable limits, of our appetitive nature, there ought to be no objection on the part of the moralist to their employment for the purpose of designating the test of right conduct; and, any way, they are useful as supplementing, correcting, and elevating the associations attached to the more commonly employed terms, pleasure and happiness. But are there no terms by which the somewhat exclusive associations connected with the two sets of phrases already examined may be avoided? I venture to suggest that such terms may be found by reverting to the old, but now usually discarded, expressions 'welfare' and 'well-being.' These words, it seems to me, do not primarily suggest material prosperity, like happiness, nor the gratification of the lower parts of our nature, like pleasure, nor the exclusive development of the higher parts of our nature, like perfection, but cover the whole ground of healthy human activity and the conditions which are favourable to it. Corresponding, too, almost exactly with the [Greek: eudaimonia] of Aristotle, they have the advantage of venerable historic associations. Lastly, they seem to have less of a personal and more of a social reference than any of the other terms employed. We speak, I think, more naturally of the well-being or welfare of society, than of the happiness, pleasure, or perfection of society. I cannot, therefore, but think that the moralist would be wise in at least trying the experiment of recurring to these terms in place of those which, in recent systems of ethics, have usually superseded them. If it be said that they are vague, and that different people will attach different meanings to them, according to their own prepossessions and their own theories of life, I can only reply that this objection applies with at least equal force to any of the other terms which we have passed in review. And, if it be said that our conceptions of well-being and welfare are not fixed, but that our ideas of the nature and proper proportions of their constituents are undergoing constant modification and growth, I may ask if this is less the case with regard to happiness, or the sum of pleasures, or the balance of pleasures over pains, or the perfection or due development of human character, all of which expressions, indeed, when properly qualified and explained, I acknowledge to be the equivalents of those for which I have stated a preference. And here occurs a difficulty with respect to all these expressions and ideas. If their meaning or content is not fixed, and specially if they are undergoing a constant change, in the way of growth, with the progress of reason and society, how can we employ them as a test of morality, which is itself also a variable conception? Surely this is to make one indefinite idea the gauge of another indefinite idea. The answer to this question will, I trust, bring out clearly the nature of a moral test, as well as the different modes of its application.

The ultimate origin of moral rules, I conceive, so far at least as science can trace them, is to be found in the effort of men to adapt themselves to the circumstances, social and physical, in which they are placed. At first, probably, this process of adaptation was almost automatic and unconscious, but, when men once began consciously to adapt means to ends, they would soon begin to reflect on their acts, and to ask themselves the reasons why they had selected this course of conduct rather than another. The justifying reasons of their past acts, like the impelling motives of their future acts, could have reference to nothing but the convenience or gratification of themselves or those amongst whom they lived. And the acts which they justified in themselves they would approve of in others. Here, then, already we have a test consciously applied to the estimation of conduct. Experience shews that this or that action promotes some object which is included in the narrow conception of well-being entertained by the primitive man. He, therefore, continues to act in accordance with the rule which prescribes it, or the habit from which it proceeds. And, in like manner, if he finds from experience that the action does not promote that object, and he is free to exercise his own choice, he desists from it and, perhaps, tries the experiment of substituting another. Now, in these cases, it is plain that any judgment which the man exercises independently, and apart from the society of which he is a member, is guided solely by the consideration whether the course of conduct is efficacious in attaining its end, that end being part of his conception of the well-being of himself, his family, or his tribe. If he thinks about the matter for himself at all, this is the only consideration of which he can take account. There are three courses open to him. He need not reflect on the action at all, but simply follow in the wake of his neighbours (and this, of course, is far the commonest case); or, if there is any divergence of opinion about it amongst his neighbours, he may deliberate as to whose opinion it is safest to follow; or, lastly, he may consider for himself, whether the action is really the best means of attaining the end aimed at, that is to say, he may test the means by its conduciveness to the end, which is always, in some shape, the welfare of himself or others. If he follows the opinion of others, it is plain that their opinion, so far as it has been formed independently, has been formed in the manner above described. The only alternative, therefore, is between the acceptance of existing opinions, without any consideration or examination, and their reference to the conception of well-being, or however else the idea may be expressed, as a measure of their appropriateness and sufficiency. The idea of well-being itself may be inadequate, and even in parts incorrect, and, as society advances, it is undoubtedly undergoing a constant process of expansion and rectification; but it seems to me that this regard for their own welfare or that of others, however we may phrase it, is the only guiding-principle of conduct, in the light of which men can reconsider and review their rules. Unless they follow the mere blind impulses of feeling (in which case they do not follow rules at all, but simply act irrationally), or else observe implicitly the maxims of conduct which they find prevalent around them, they must, and can only, ask the question whether it is possible to alter their conduct for the better, that is to say, whether they can better promote their own welfare or that of others by some modification of their actions. Take the case of Slavery. There was a time when savage or barbaric tribes, moved by a regard to their own interests, and also, we may trust, touched by some compassion for their victims, began to substitute, for the wholesale butchery of their enemies defeated in war, the practice of retaining some or all of them for the purposes of domestic or agrarian service. Again, there came a time when, viewed by the side of other forms of service which had meanwhile come into existence, slavery, with its various incidents, began to shock the philanthropic sentiments of the more civilized races of mankind, while the question also began to be raised whether slave-labour was not economically at a disadvantage, when compared with free labour, and the result of these combined considerations, often aided by a strong and enthusiastic outburst of popular feeling, has been the total disappearance of slavery amongst civilized, and its almost total disappearance even amongst barbaric or semi-civilized races. Take, too, the revolting practice, common among many savage tribes, past and present, of killing and eating aged parents or other infirm members of the tribe, when engaged in war. This practice which, at first sight, seems so utterly unnatural, was doubtless dictated, in part at least, by the desire to save their victims from the worse fate of being tortured and mutilated by their enemies. Subsequently, in the history of some of these tribes, there has come a time when it has been discovered that a more humane mode of attaining the same object is to build strong places and leave the feebler folk at home. If we follow the varying marriage customs of savage or barbaric tribes, we shall find, in the same way, that they have always been originally framed on reasons of convenience, and that, when they have been changed, it has been because different views of well-being, including the needs of purity, closer attachment, increased care of children, and the like, have begun to prevail. In all these examples, which might be multiplied to any extent, it is plain that changes of conduct are moulded and determined by changes of opinion as to what is best and most suitable for the circumstances of the individual, the family, the tribe, or whatever the social aggregate may be. And I may venture to affirm that, wherever any change of moral conduct takes place, unless it be dictated by blind passion, or mere submission to authority, enforced or voluntary, the change is invariably due to some change of opinion on what constitutes the advantage of the persons whom it affects. It is true, therefore, that moral conduct varies, and it is true that our conceptions of well-being vary, but the two do not vary independently of one another, or either of them capriciously. Increased experience of ourselves and of others, enlarged observation of the external world, more matured reflexion are constantly expanding and rectifying our conceptions of what constitutes human welfare, and to this constantly amended conception are readjusted, from time to time, our conduct and our sentiments on the conduct both of ourselves and of others. In brief, then, the conduct of men and the sentiments of men on conduct vary with their conceptions of well-being, and their conceptions of well-being are determined by experience (including the opportunity for experience) and reflexion.

My conclusion may, perhaps, be illustrated and enforced by one further consideration. It generally happens, in the progress of society, that, after a number of rules of conduct have been accumulated, they become enshrined in some sacred book, some code, or, at least, some constant and authoritative tradition. In this manner they may be stereotyped for ages. Now, after a time, these rules, especially if they are numerous and minute, become unsuited, at least in part, to the altered circumstances of the society, and probably bear hardly on many of the individuals composing it. When this condition of things is beginning to be intolerable, there often arises the social reformer, and what is the course which he pursues? He endeavours to shew how unsuitable the rules have become to attain the ends which they were originally intended to compass, in how much better a manner other rules would attain these objects, how grievously the present rules bear on many classes and individuals in the state, how unequal they are in their incidence, at what a disadvantage they place the community in comparison with neighbouring communities, how easily they may be altered, and the like. In fact, the considerations which he urges may all be included in the one argument that the existing rules are opposed to the well-being of the state, and that the advantages resulting from their abrogation will more than compensate for any disturbance of existing relations which may ensue from the change. Apart from force, or mere rant, rhetoric, or imposture, it is difficult to see what other resource the reformer has open to him. And, in those cases where there is no accumulation of antiquated rules and no need of the individual reformer, but where society at large has the happy knack of imperceptibly accommodating its practice and principles of action to altered circumstances, there can be no doubt that it is by considerations of well-being, half conscious though the process of application may be, that the change is directed. The plastic power by which men accommodate their actions and even their maxims of conduct to modifications in surrounding circumstances is one of the advantages which they gain by the progress of civilisation. In ancient society the tyranny of custom is often almost absolute. In modern society changes, which would otherwise require the drastic hand of the reformer, are often quietly effected by the gradual and almost imperceptible action of the people themselves. It is thus that the equity branch of English law, and much of our case law, grew up, giving expression to changes which had already occurred in the current of popular opinion. It is thus that the obligation of 'gentlemen' to offer, on the slightest provocation, and to accept, without questioning, a 'challenge' to take each other's lives, has, in most civilized countries, now grown obsolete, having gradually become enfeebled together with the exaggerated military spirit which gave it birth. It is thus also that, with an increase of the industrial spirit, with softened manners, and with that quickening of our sympathetic nature which has gradually been effected by the teaching of Christianity, a strong sentiment against slavery, a respect for human life as such, a regard for the weak, the suffering, the oppressed, and many tender feelings of a similar kind, have almost insensibly been developed as an essential element in modern civilisation.

These considerations naturally lead me to notice the two different ways in which the test of conduct may be, and as a fact is, applied. One mode is the conscious and intentional application of it by the reflective man. The other is the semi-conscious and almost instinctive application of it by the community at large. In morals, as in the arts, men, almost without knowing it, are constantly re-adjusting their means to their ends, feeling their way to some tentative solution of a new difficulty or a better solution of an old one, shaping their conduct with reference to the special needs of the situation in which they are placed. It is thus, for the most part, that new circumstances develop new rules, and that the simple maxims of a primitive people are gradually replaced by the multifarious code of law and morals with which we are now familiar. The guiding principle throughout the process is the conception of their own good, comprehending, as it does, not only ease, personal comfort, and gratification of the various appetites and desires, which, in the early stages of society, are the preponderating considerations, but also those higher constituents of welfare, both individual and social, which attain an ever-increasing importance as society advances, such as are the development of the moral, the intellectual, and the aesthetic faculties; the purification of the religious sentiments, the expansion of the sympathetic feelings, the diffusion of liberty and prosperity, the consolidation of national unity, the elevation of human life. This principle works throughout the community, actuating some men in its higher, others in its lower forms; but, except where the force of tradition or prejudice is too strong for it, invariably moulding conduct into accordance with the more complex requirements of advancing civilisation. Its action, of course, is not wholly advantageous. Growing needs and more complicated relations suggest to men fresh devices for compassing their selfish ends, such as the various forms of fraud, forgery, and conspiracy, as well as more enlarged or more effective schemes of beneficence, stricter or more intelligent applications of the principle of justice, and possibilities of higher and freer developments of their faculties. But, on the whole, and setting aside as exceptional certain periods of retrogression, such as the decline of the Roman Empire, the evolution of society seems to be attended by the progress of morality, and specially by the amelioration of social relations, whether between individuals, families, or states. The intelligence that apprehends the greater good re-acts upon the desire to attain it, and the result is the combination of more rational aims with a purer interest in the pursuit of them.

This tendency in society at large to modify and re-adjust its conduct in conformity with fuller and more improved conceptions of well-being, which are themselves suggested by a growing experience, is reinforced, especially in the later stages of civilisation, by the consciously reflective action of philosophers and reformers. It is the function of these classes not only to give expression to the thoughts which are working obscurely in the minds of other men, but also to detect those aspects and bearings of conduct which are not obvious to the general intelligence. This task is effected partly by tracing actions to their indirect and remote results, partly by more distinctly realising their results, whether immediate or remote, direct or indirect, and partly by generalising them, that is to say, by considering what would happen to society if men generally were to act in that manner. Thus, take the case of lying. In primitive states of society, and even in some more advanced nations, no great opprobrium attaches to telling a lie. In ancient Greece, for instance, veracity by no means occupied the same prominent position among the virtues that it does among ourselves, and, even now, Teutonic races are generally credited with a peculiar sensitiveness on the subject of truthfulness. This improved sentiment as regards veracity is, no doubt, partly due to the realisation of its importance and of the inconveniences which result from the breaches of it, especially in commercial affairs, by the members of a community at large, but it must also, to a great extent, have been produced by the definite teaching conveyed in books, and by moral and religious instructors. Follow out a lie to all its consequences, realise the feelings of the person deceived by it, when he has discovered the deception, above all, consider what would be the result if men were commonly to deceive one another, and no man could place any dependence on the information which his neighbour gave him; and then a falsehood excites very different feelings from what it does when regarded simply as an isolated act. Or, again, take the evasion of taxes. There is probably, even yet, no country in which the popular sentiment on this subject is sufficiently enlightened and severe. A man smuggles a box of cigars, or evades paying a tax for his dog, or makes an insufficient return of his income, and few of his neighbours, if the fact come to their knowledge, think the worse of him. The character and consequences of the action are not obvious, and hence they do not perceive what, on reflexion, or, if guided by proper instruction, they could hardly fail to realise, that the act is really a theft, only practised on the community at large instead of on an individual member of it, and that, if every one were to act in the same way, the collection of taxes and, consequently, the administration and defence of the country, the maintenance of its army and navy, its police, its harbours and roads, would become an impossibility, and it would quickly relapse into barbarism. Other familiar instances of the advantage to be derived from the conscious and intentional application of the reasoning powers to matters of conduct may be found in the successive reforms of the penal code of any civilized country, or in the abolition of slavery. Punishment is, in all very early stages of society, capricious, mostly unregulated by any definite customs or enactments, and, consequently, often disproportioned, either in the way of excess or defect, to the character of the offence. As the community advances in complexity and intelligence, successive reformers arise who attempt, by definite enactment, to regulate the amount of punishment due to each description of offence, and, from time to time, to increase or diminish, as occasion seems to require, the severity of the existing code. The considerations by which, at least in our own time, these reforms are determined are such as these: the adequacy or inadequacy of the punishment to deter men from the commission of the offence, the tendency of excessive punishment to produce a reaction of sentiment in favour of the criminal, and a reluctance on the part of the judge or jury to convict, the superfluous suffering inflicted by that part of the punishment which is in excess of the requirements of the case, due publicity and notoriety as a means of warning others, the reform of the criminal himself, and so on. All these considerations, it will be observed, are derived from tracing the effects of the punishment either on the criminal himself, or on persons who are under a similar temptation to commit the crime, or on the sentiment of society at large, or of that portion of society which is connected with the administration of justice, and it is only by the exercise of great circumspection, and of a keen intelligence on the part of the statesman, the jurist, or the moralist, that grave errors can be avoided, and an adequate estimate of the probable results can be formed. The mere instinct of the community, unmodified and uncorrected by the conscious speculations of its more thoughtful members, would be in much danger of either causing a large amount of needless suffering to the criminal, or of seriously diminishing the security of society. It would almost certainly be guilty of grave inequalities in the apportionment of punishment to specific crimes. The history of slavery similarly shews the importance of the functions of the moralist and the reformer. It must have been at the suggestion of some prominent member of a tribe, whose intelligence was in advance of that of his fellows, that men first took to capturing their defeated enemies, with a view to future service, instead of slaughtering them on the field of battle. And we know that, in the time of Plato and Aristotle, there had already arisen a strong sentiment against the enslaving of Greeks by Greeks, originating probably in the instinctive sympathy of race, but quickened and fostered, doubtless, by the superior capacity which men possess of realising suffering and misfortune in those who are constituted and endowed like themselves, by the new conception of a Pan-hellenic unity, and by the vivid sense which, on reflexion, the citizens of each state must have entertained of their own liability to be reduced, in turn, to the same condition. In modern times, the movement which has led to the entire abolition of slavery in civilized countries owes much, undoubtedly, to the softened manners and wider sympathies of a society largely transformed by the combined operation of Christianity and culture, but it has been promoted, to no inconsiderable degree, by conscious reflexion and direct argument. Social and religious reasons, derived from the community of nature and origin in man, reinforced by a vivid realisation of the sufferings of others, and appealing forcibly to the tender and sympathetic feelings, have co-operated with the economical considerations drawn from the wastefulness and comparative inefficiency of slave labour, and with what may be called the self-regarding reason of the hardening and debasing effect of slave-owning on the character of the slave-owner himself.

It will be sufficient, in this connexion, simply to allude to the ideals of mercy, purity, humility, long-suffering, and self-denial, which are pourtrayed in the Christian teaching and have, ever since the early days of Christianity, exercised so vast and powerful an influence on large sections of mankind.

There is, of course, a process of constant Interaction going on between the two elements in the constitution of moral sentiment which I have been attempting to describe. The circumstances, opinions, and feelings of the society of which he is a member, must necessarily contribute to determine the opinions and feelings, the character and aims, of the moralist or the reformer. In turn, the moralist or reformer modifies, corrects, and elevates the current moral sentiment of those who are brought within the influence of his work. And this result is usually a permanent one. When the average moral sentiment on a particular point of conduct has been consciously raised, and the change is fully realised, it seldom happens that it afterwards recedes, though the automatic or semi-conscious adaptations of society to new needs and circumstances, when regarded from a more general point of view, are not infrequently found to be regressive as well as progressive. Thus, though we may imagine the distinctions between the different classes of society becoming more numerous or more accentuated (as I believe to have actually occurred in England during the present century), or the evasion of taxation becoming more general than it at present is, we can hardly conceive a recurrence to slavery, or a needless increase in the severity of punishments, or a revival of the hard-drinking habits of the last century. When society is fully aware of its moral gains, it is not likely knowingly to surrender them. Hence, allowing for occasional oscillations and for possible exceptions in certain departments of conduct, morality, as a whole, almost necessarily advances with the general progress of intelligence.

It is not altogether easy to adjust the respective claims of society at large and of the individual thinker in the constitution of moral theory, or, in other words, to determine the limits within which the speculative moralist may legitimately endeavour to reform the existing moral sentiment. It is plain that it must be open to the moralist, and, in fact, to every intelligent citizen, to criticize the current morality, or else moral progress, even if it took place at all, would, on many points of conduct, be exceedingly slow. But, on the other hand, it is equally plain that a constant discussion of the accepted rules of conduct would weaken the moral sentiment, lessen the sense of obligation, and suggest a general uncertainty as to the validity of the maxims which, in their relations to one another, men usually take for granted. Hence, though it would be almost fatal to moral progress to discourage speculation on moral topics, the moralist must always bear in mind that his task is one which is not lightly to be undertaken, and that, with an exception to be noticed presently, the presumption should always be in favour of existing rules of conduct. If for no other reason, this presumption ought to be made on the practical ground that a disturbance of the moral sentiment on one point is likely to weaken its force generally, and, before we expose men to this danger, we ought to have some adequate justification. But there is also the speculative ground that any given society, and indeed mankind generally, has been engaged for ages in feeling its way, instinctively or semi-consciously, towards a solution of the self-same problems which the philosopher is attempting to solve consciously and of set purpose. That, on the whole, a society has solved these problems in the manner best suited to its existing needs and circumstances may fairly be taken for granted, and, even where the ethical stand-point of the reformer is very superior to the stand-point of the society which he wishes to reform, he will be wise in endeavouring to introduce his reforms gradually, and, if possible, in connexion with principles already acknowledged, rather than in attempting to effect a moral revolution, the ultimate results of which it may be impossible to foresee. The work of the moralist is, therefore, best regarded as corrective of, and supplementary to, the work which mankind is constantly doing for itself, and not as antagonistic to it. The method is the same in both cases: only it is applied semi-consciously, and merely as occasions suggest it, in the one case; consciously and spontaneously in the other. In both cases alike the guiding principle, whether of action or of speculation upon action, is the adaptation of conduct to surrounding circumstances, physical and social, with a view to promote, to the utmost extent possible, the well-being of the individual and of the society of which he is a member. Where the interests of the individual and of the society clash, society, that is to say, a man's fellow-citizens, usually approves, as we saw in the last chapter, of the sacrifice of individual to social interests, a course of conduct which is also, on reflexion, usually stamped by the individual's own approbation, and hence we may say briefly that their tendency to promote or impair the welfare of society is the test by which, in different ways, all actions are estimated alike by the philosopher, in his hours of speculation, and by the community at large, in the practical work of life.

In laying down the principle that the presumption of the moralist should always be in favour of existing rules of conduct, I intimated that there was one exception to this principle. The exception includes all those cases which are legitimate, though not obvious, applications of existing rules, and to which, therefore, the ordinary moral sentiment does not attach in the same way that it does to the plainer and more direct applications. Thus, if it can be shewn, as it undoubtedly can be, that smuggling falls under the head of stealing, and holding out false hopes under that of lying, the moralist need take no account of the lax moral sentiment which exists with regard to these practices, though, of course, in estimating the guilt of the individual as distinct from the character of the act, due allowance must be made for his imperfect appreciation of the moral bearings of his conduct. This exception, as will be found in the next chapter, covers, and therefore at once justifies, a large proportion of the criticisms which, in the present advanced stage of morality, when the more fundamental principles have been already settled, it is still open to us to make.

It remains now to enquire what is the justification of the test propounded in this chapter. I do not found it on any external considerations, whether of Law or Revelation, both of which, I conceive, presuppose morality, but on the very make and constitution of our nature. The justification of the moral test and the source of the moral feeling are alike, I conceive, to be discovered by an examination of human nature, and, so far as that nature has a divine origin, so far is the origin of morality divine. Whatever the ultimate source of morality may be, to us, at all events, it can only be known as revealed or reflected in ourselves. What, then, is it in the constitution of our nature, which leads us to aim at the well-being of ourselves and those around us, and to measure our own conduct and that of others by the extent to which it promotes these ends? In answering this question, I must give a brief account of the ultimate principles of human nature, though this account has been partly anticipated in the last chapter. Human nature, in its last analysis, seems, so far as it is concerned with action, to consist of certain impulses or feelings, and a power of comparing with one another the results which follow from the gratification of these feelings, which power reacts upon the several feelings themselves by way of intensifying, checking, or controlling them. This power we call Reason. The feelings themselves fall into two principal groups, the egoistic or self-regarding feelings, which centre in a man's self, and are developed by his personal needs, and the altruistic or sympathetic feelings, which centre in others and are developed by the social surroundings in which he finds himself placed. These two groups of feelings, I conceive, were independent of one another from the first, or at least as soon as man could be called man, and neither of them admits of being resolved into the other. As the one was developed by and adapted to personal needs, so the other was developed by and adapted to the manifold requirements of family or tribal life, which, from the first, was inseparable from the life of the individual. Intermediate between these two groups of feelings, the purely self-regarding and the purely sympathetic, and derived probably from the interaction of both, is another group, which may be called the semi-social group. This group includes shame, love of reputation, love of notoriety, desire of fame, and the like, but, on analysis, it will be found that all these feelings admit of being referred to two heads, the love of approbation and the fear of disapprobation. Lastly, if any of our desires or feelings are thwarted by the intentional action of other men, the result in our minds is a feeling which we call Resentment, and which, though it regards others, is, unlike the sympathetic feelings, a malevolent and not a benevolent feeling. It is important, in considering the economy of human nature, to notice that Resentment, as is also the case with the love of cruelty, is a secondary not a primary, a derived not an original affection of our minds; for, apart from the desire to gratify some self-regarding or sympathetic feeling, or disappointment when that desire is not gratified, there is, I conceive, no such thing as ill-feeling in one human being towards another. Resentment is properly a reflex form of sympathy or self-regard, arising when our sympathetic feelings are wounded by an injury done to another, or our self-regarding desires are frustrated by an injury done to ourselves; when, in fact, any emotional element in our nature is, by the intentional intervention of another, disappointed of attaining its end. Each of these groups of feelings admits of being studied apart, though in the actual conduct of life they are seldom found to operate alone, and each, under the continued action of reason, assumes a form or forms in which its various elements are brought into harmonious working with each other, so as best to promote the ends which the whole group subserves. These forms, thus rationalised or moralised, if I may be allowed the use of such expressions, are, in the case of the self-regarding feelings, self-respect and rational self-love; in the case of the sympathetic feelings, rational benevolence; in the case of the semi-social feelings, a reasonable regard for the opinion of others; and in the case of the resentful feelings, a sense of justice. These higher forms of the several groups of feelings themselves require to be harmonised, before man can satisfy the needs of his nature as a whole. And, when co-ordinated under the control of reason, they become a rational desire for the combined welfare of the individual and of society, or, if we choose to use different but equivalent expressions, of the individual considered as an unit of society, or of society considered as including the individual. In a settled state of existence, the interests of the individual and of society, even leaving out of account the pleasures and pains of the moral sanction, are, for the most part, identical. If an individual pursues a selfish course of conduct, neglecting the interests and feelings of others, he is almost certain to suffer for it in the long run. And the prosperity and general well-being of the community in which they live is, to citizens, living a normal life and pursuing ordinary avocations, an essential condition of their own prosperity and well-being. On the other hand, it is by each man attending to his own business and directing his efforts to the promotion of his own interests or those of his family, his firm, or whatever may be the smaller social aggregate in which his work chiefly lies, that the interests of the community at large are best secured. Men whose time is mainly taken up with philanthropic enterprises are very likely to neglect the duties which lie immediately before them. 'To learn and labour truly to get mine own living, and to do my duty in that state of life, unto which it shall please God to call me' is a very homely, but it is an essential lesson. That the great mass of the citizens of a country should lay it well to heart, and act habitually on it, is the first condition of national prosperity. Of course, this primary regard to our own interests, or those of the persons with whom we are more immediately connected, must be limited by wider considerations. A man has duties, not only to himself and his own family, but to his neighbours, to the various institutions with which he is connected, to his town, his country, mankind at large, and even the whole sentient creation. How far these should limit each other or a man's individual or family interests is a question by no means easy to answer, and is the main problem which each man has to be perpetually solving for himself, and society at large for us all. There is hardly any waking hour in which we have not to attempt to settle rival claims of this kind, and, according as we settle them to our own satisfaction or not, so have we peace or trouble of mind. No one can reasonably deny that the more immediate interests of the individual and of the various social aggregates, including society at large, are frequently in conflict. It seems to me, I must confess, that it is also futile to deny that there are occasions, though such occasions may be rare, in which even a man's interests in the long run are incompatible with his social duties. To take one or two instances. It may sometimes be for the good of society that a man should speak out his mind freely on some question of private conduct or public policy, though his utterances may be on the unpopular side or offend persons of consideration and influence. The man performs what he conceives to be his duty, but he knows that, in doing so, he is sacrificing his prospects. Or, again, he is invited to join in some popular movement which he believes to be of a questionable or pernicious tendency, and, because he believes that to take part in it would be untrue to his own convictions and possibly harmful to others, he refrains from doing so, at the risk of losing preferment, or custom, or patronage. Then, we are all familiar with the difficulties in which men are often placed, when they have to record a vote; their convictions and the claims of the public service being on one side, and their own interests and prospects on the other. In all these cases it is true that, if their moral nature be in a healthy condition, they approve, on reflexion, of having taken the more generous course, while it is often a matter of life-long regret if they have sacrificed their nobler impulses to their selfish interests. And, taking into account these after-feelings of self-approbation and self-disapprobation, it is often the case, and is always the case where these feelings are very strong, that a man gains more happiness, in the long run, by following the path of duty and obeying his social impulses than by confining himself to the narrow view which would be dictated by a cool calculation of what is most likely to conduce to his own private good. But, where the moral feelings are not strong, and still more where they are almost in abeyance, I fear that the theory that virtue and happiness are invariably coincident will hardly be supported by a candid examination of facts. To some men, I fear it must be acknowledged, present wealth and power and dignity are more than a sufficient recompense for any remorse which they may continue to feel for past greed or lack of candour or truthfulness. These considerations will serve to shew the immense importance of moral education, alike in the family, the school, and the state. If we are to depend on men acting rightly, and with a due regard to wider interests than their own, we must take pains to develop in them moral feelings sufficiently strong and sensitive to make the reflexion on wrong or selfish acts more painful to them than the sacrifice which is needed for dutiful and generous conduct. So far as society, through its various instruments of law and opinion, of education and domestic influences, can effect this object, so far will it promote its own security and advancement.

Our adoption, then, of a tendency to promote social welfare or well-being, as the test of conduct, is justified, I conceive, by an examination of the internal constitution of human nature and of the conditions which are necessary to secure the harmonious working of its various parts. It may be objected that this test is vague in its conception and difficult in its application. Both objections, to a great extent, hold good. If they did not, moral theory and moral practice would be very easy matters, but, as a fact, we know that they are by no means easy. The conception of social well-being must be more or less vague, because we are constantly filling it up by experience; it is not a fixed, but a growing conception, and, though we may be certain of the character and importance of many of the elements which have already been detected in it by the experience of past generations, it seems impossible to fix any limits to its development in the future history of mankind. Man will constantly be discovering new wants, new and more refined susceptibilities of his nature, and with them his conception of human well-being must necessarily grow. But, though not a fixed or final conception, the idea of social well-being is sufficiently definite, in each generation, to act as a guide and incentive to conduct. It is the star, gradually growing brighter and brighter, which lights our path, and, any way, we know that, if it were not above us in the heavens, we should be walking in the darkness.

It must be confessed that the test of social well-being is not always easy of application. Even, when we know what the good of the community consists in, it is not always easy to say what course of action will promote it, or what course of action is likely to retard it. Society arrives, in a comparatively early period of its development, at certain broad rules of conduct, such as those which condemn murder, theft, ingratitude to friends, disobedience to parents. But the more remote applications of these rules, the nicer shades of conduct, such as those relating to social intercourse, the choice between clashing duties, the realisation of our obligations to the community at large, require for their appreciation a large amount of intelligence and an accumulated stock of experience which are not to be found in primitive societies. Hence, the rules of conduct, which at first are few and simple, gradually become more numerous and complex. Nor have we yet arrived at the time, nor do we seem to be within any appreciable distance of it, when the code is complete, or even the parts of it which already exist are altogether free from doubt and discussion. In the simpler relations of life, he that runs may read, but with increasing complications comes increasing uncertainty. To remove, as far as may be, this uncertainty from the domain of conduct is the task of advancing civilisation, and specially of those members of a community who have sufficient leisure, education, and intelligence to review the motives and compare the results of actions. The task has doubtless its special difficulties, and the conclusions of the moralist will by no means always command assent, but that the art of life is an easy one, who is there, at all experienced in affairs or accustomed to reflexion, that will contend?

I may here pause for a moment, in order to emphasise the fact, which is already abundantly apparent from what has preceded, that, with ever widening and deepening conceptions of well-being, man is constantly learning to subordinate his individual interests to those of society at large, or rather to identify his interests with those of the larger organism of which he is a part. It is thus that we may justify the peculiar characteristic of the moral sentiment, indicated in the last chapter, which seems, in all acts of which it approves, to demand an element of sacrifice, whether of the lower to the higher self, or of the individual to his fellows. In order thoroughly to realise ourselves, we must be conscious of our absorption, or at least of our inclusion, in a greater and grander system than that of our individual surroundings; in order to find our lives, we must first discover the art of losing them.

CHAPTER V.
PRACTICAL APPLICATIONS OF THE MORAL TEST.

In this chapter I propose, without any attempt to be exhaustive or systematic, to give some examples of the manner in which the test of conduct may be applied to practical questions, either by extending existing rules to cases which do not obviously fall under them, or by suggesting more refined maxims of conduct than those which are commonly prevalent. In either case, I am accepting the somewhat invidious task of pointing out defects in the commonly received theory, or the commonly approved practice, of morality. But, if morality is progressive, as I contend that it is, and progresses by the application to conduct of a test which itself involves a growing conception, the best mode of exhibiting the application of that test will be in the more recent acquisitions or the more subtle deductions of morality, rather than in its fundamental rules or most acknowledged maxims.

I shall begin with a topic, the examples of which are ready to hand, and may easily be multiplied, to almost any extent, by the reader for himself--the better realisation of our duties to society at large as distinct from particular individuals. When the primary mischief resulting from a wrong act falls upon individuals, and especially upon our neighbours or those with whom we are constantly associating, it can hardly escape our observation. And, even if it does, the probability is that our attention will be quickly called to it by the reprobation of others. But, when the consequences of the act are diffused over the whole community, or a large aggregate of persons, so that the effect on each individual is almost imperceptible, we are very apt to overlook the mischief resulting from it, and so not to recognise its wrongful character, while, at the same time, from lack of personal interest, others fail to call us to account. Hence it is that men, almost without any thought, and certainly often without any scruple, commit offences against the public or against corporations or societies or companies, which they would themselves deem it impossible for them to commit against individuals. And yet the character of the acts is exactly the same. Take smuggling. A man smuggles cigars or tobacco to an amount by which he saves himself twenty shillings, and defrauds the state to the same extent. This is simply an act of theft, only that the object of the theft is the community at large and not an individual. So far as the mischief or wrongfulness of the act goes, apart from the intention of the agent, he might as well put his hands into the pocket of one of his fellow-passengers and extract the same amount of money. The twenty shillings which, by evading payment of the duty, he has appropriated to his own uses, has been taken from the rest of the tax-payers, and he has simply shifted on to them the obligation which properly attached to himself. Sooner or later they must make up the deficit. If many men were to act in the same way, the burden of the honest tax-payer would be largely increased, and, if the practice became general, the state would have to resort to some other mode of taxation or collect its customs-revenue at a most disproportionate cost. Thus, a little reflexion shows that smuggling is really theft, and I cannot but think that it would be to the moral as well as the material advantage of the community if it were called by that name, and were visited with the same punishment as petty larceny. Exactly the same remarks, of course, apply to the evasion of income-tax, or of rates or taxes of any kind, which are imposed by a legitimate authority. Travelling on a railway without a ticket or in a higher class or for a greater distance than that for which the ticket was taken is, similarly, only a thinly disguised case of theft, and should be treated accordingly. The sale or purchase of pirated editions of books is another case of the same kind, the persons from whom the money is stolen being the authors or publishers. Many paltry acts of pilfering, such as the unauthorised use of government-paper or franks, or purloining novels or letter-paper from a club, or plucking flowers in a public garden, fall under the same head of real, though not always obvious, thefts. There is, of course, a certain degree of pettiness which makes them insignificant, but there is always a danger lest men should think too lightly of acts of this kind, whether done by themselves or others. The best safeguard, perhaps, against thoughtless wrong-doing to the community or large social aggregates is to ask ourselves these two questions:

Should we commit this act, or what should we think of a man who did commit it, in the case of a private individual? What would be the result, if every one who had the opportunity were to do the same? Many of these acts would, then, stand out in their true light, and we should recognise that they are not only mean but criminal.

Other, but analogous, instances of the failure of men to realise their obligations to society or to large social aggregates are to be found in the careless and perfunctory manner in which persons employed by government, or by corporations, or large companies, often perform their duties. If they were in the service of a private employer, they would at all events realise, even if they did not act on their conviction, that they were defrauding him by idling away their time or attending to their own affairs, or those of charities or institutions in which they were interested, when they ought to be attending to the concerns of their employer. But in a government or municipal office, or the establishment of a large company, no one in particular seems to be injured by the ineffective discharge of their functions; and hence it does not occur to them that they are receiving their wages without rendering the equivalent of them. The inadequate supervision which overlooks or condones this listlessness is, of course, itself also the result of a similar failure to realise responsibility.

The spirit in which patronage is often administered affords an instance of a similar kind. If a man were engaging a person to perform some service for himself or his family, or one of his intimate friends, he would simply look to competency, including, perhaps, moral character, for the special work to be done. But, when he has to appoint to a public post, and especially if he is only one of a board of electors, he is very apt to think that there is no great harm in appointing or voting for a relative or friend, or a person who has some special bond of connexion with him, such as that of political party, though he may not be the candidate best qualified for the position. And, if it does occur to him that he is acting wrongly, he is more likely to think of the wrong which he is doing to the individual who possesses the highest qualifications (and to him it is an undoubted wrong, for it frustrates just expectations) than of the wrong which he is doing to the community or the institution which he is depriving of the services of the fittest man. And yet, if he takes the trouble to reflect, he must see that he is guilty of a breach of trust; that, having undertaken a public duty, he has abused the confidence reposed in him.

A vote given in return for a bribe, a case which now seldom occurs except in parliamentary elections, is open to the same ethical objections as a vote given on grounds of partiality; and, as the motive which dictates the breach of trust is purely selfish, it incurs the additional reproach of meanness. But why, it may be asked, should not a man accept a bribe, if, on other grounds, he would vote for the candidate who offers it? Simply, because he is encouraging a practice which would, in time, deprive Parliament of most of its more competent members, and reduce it to an oligarchy of millionaires, as well as degrading himself by a sordid act. To receive a present for a vote, even if the vote be given conscientiously, is to lend countenance to a practice which must inevitably corrupt the consciences, and pervert the judgment, of others. It hardly needs to be pointed out that the man who offers the bribe is acting still more immorally than the man who accepts it. He is not only causing others to act immorally, but, as no man can be a proper judge of his own competency, he is attempting to thrust himself into an office of trust without any regard to his fitness to fill it. Intimidation, on the part of the man who practises it, is on the same ethical level as bribery, with respect to the two points just mentioned; but, as it appeals to the fears of men instead of their love of gain, and costs nothing to him who employs it, it is more odious, and deserves, at the hands of the law, a still more severe punishment. To yield to intimidation is, under most circumstances, more excusable than to yield to bribery; for the fear of losing what one has is to most men a more powerful inducement than the hope of gaining what one has not, and, generally speaking, the penalty threatened by the intimidator is far in excess of the advantage offered by the briber.

As it betrays a vain and grasping disposition, when a man attempts to thrust himself into an office to which he is not called by the spontaneous voice of his fellow-citizens, so to refuse office, when there is an evident opportunity of doing good service to the community, betrays pride or indolence, coupled with an indifference to the public welfare. In democratic communities, there is always a tendency on the part of what may be called superfine persons to hold aloof from public, and especially municipal, life. If this sentiment of fastidiousness or indifference were to spread widely, and a fashion which begins in one social stratum quickly permeates to those immediately below it, there would be great danger, as there seems to be in America, of the public administration becoming seriously and permanently deteriorated. To prevent this evil, it is desirable to create, in every community, a strong sentiment against the practice of persons, who have the requisite means, leisure, and ability, withholding themselves from public life, when invited by their fellow-citizens to take their part in it. There may, of course, be paramount claims of another kind, such as those of science, or art, or literature, or education, but the superior importance of these claims on the individuals themselves, where they obviously exist, and where the claims of the public service are not urgent, would readily be allowed.

It seems to be a rapid transition from cases of this kind to suicide, but, amongst the many reasons, moral and religious, which may be urged against suicide, there is one which connects itself closely with the considerations which have just been under our notice. As pointed out long ago by Aristotle, the suicide wrongs the state rather than himself. Where a man is still able to do any service to the state, in either a private or a public capacity, he is under a social, and, therefore, a moral obligation to perform that service, and, consequently, to withdraw from it by a voluntary death is to desert the post of duty. This consideration, of course, holds only where a man's life is still of value to society, but it should be pointed out that, where this ceases to be the case, many other considerations often, and some always do, intervene. There are few men who have not relatives, friends, or neighbours, who will be pained, even if they are not injured materially, by an act of suicide, and, wherever the injury is a material one, as in the case of leaving helpless relatives unprovided for, it becomes an act of cruelty. Then, under all circumstances, there remain the evil example of cowardice and, to those who acknowledge the obligations of religion, the sin of cutting short the period of probation which God has assigned us.

Amongst duties to society, which are seldom fully realised in their social aspect, is the duty of bringing up children in such a manner as to render them useful to the state, instead of a burden upon it. Under this head, there are two distinct cases, that of the rich and that of the poor, or, more precisely, that of those who are in sufficiently good circumstances to educate their children without the assistance of the state or of their neighbours, and that of those who require such assistance. In the latter case, it is the duty of society to co-operate with the parent in giving the child an education which shall fit it for the industrial occupations of life, and hence the moral obligation on the richer members of a community to provide elementary schools, aided by the state or by some smaller political aggregate, or else by voluntary efforts. The object of this assistance is not so much charity to the parent or the individual children, as the prevention of crime and pauperism, and the supply of an orderly and competent industrial class. In rendering the assistance, whether it come from public or private funds, great care ought to be taken not to weaken, but, rather to stimulate, the interest of the parent in the child's progress, both by assigning to him a share of the responsibility of supervision, and, if possible, by compelling him to contribute an equitable proportion of the cost. So largely, if not so fully, are the duties of the state and of individuals of the wealthier classes, in the matter of educating the children of the poor, now recognised, that the dangers arising from a defective or injudicious education seem, in the immediate future, to threaten the richer rather than the poorer classes. Over-indulgence and the encouragement of luxurious habits during childhood; the weakened sense of responsibility, on the part of the parent, which is often caused by the transference to others of authority and supervision during boyhood or girlhood; the undue stimulation of the love of amusement, or of the craving for material comforts, during the opening years of manhood or womanhood; the failure to create serious interests or teach adequately the social responsibilities which wealth and position bring with them,--all these mistakes or defects in the education of the children of the upper classes constitute a grave peril to society, unless they are remedied in time. It seems, so far as we can forecast the future, that it is only by all classes taking pains to ascertain their respective duties and functions in sustaining and promoting the well-being of the community, and making serious efforts to perform them, that the society of the next few generations can be saved from constant convulsions. As intelligence expands, and a sense of the importance of social co-operation becomes diffused, it is almost certain that the existence of a merely idle and self-indulgent class will no longer be tolerated. Hence, it is as much to the interests of the wealthier classes themselves as of society at large, that their children should be educated with a full sense of their social responsibilities, and equipped with all the moral and intellectual aptitudes which are requisite to enable them to take a lead in the development of the community of which they are members.

And here, perhaps, I may take occasion to draw attention to the importance of the acquisition of political knowledge by all citizens of the state, and especially by those who belong to the leisured classes. It is a plain duty to society, that men should not exercise political power, unless they have some knowledge of the questions at issue. The amount of this knowledge may vary almost infinitely, from that of the veteran statesman to that of the newly enfranchised elector, but it is within the power of every one, who can observe and reason, to acquire some knowledge of at least the questions which affect his own employment and the welfare of his own family and neighbourhood, and, unless he will take thus much pains, he might surely have the modesty to forego his vote. To record a vote simply to please some one else is only one degree baser than to barter it for money or money's worth, and indeed it is often only an indirect mode of doing the same thing.

There is a large class of cases, primarily affecting individuals rather than society at large, which, if we look a little below the surface and trace their results, are of a much more pernicious character than is usually recognised, and, as ethical knowledge increases, ought to incur far more severe reprobation than they now do. Foremost amongst these is what I may call the current morality of debts. A man incurs a debt with a tradesman which he has no intention or no reasonable prospect of paying, knowing that the tradesman has no grounds for suspecting his inability to pay. The tradesman parts with the goods, supposing that he will receive the equivalent; the customer carries them off, knowing that this equivalent is not, and is not likely to be, forthcoming. I confess that I am entirely unable to distinguish this case from that of ordinary theft. And still there is many a man, well received in society, who habitually acts in this manner, and whose practice must be more than suspected by his friends and associates. He and his friends would be much astonished if he were accosted as a thief, and still I cannot see how he could reasonably repudiate this title. Short of this extreme case, which, however, is by no means uncommon, there are many degrees of what may be called criminal negligence or imprudence in contracting debts, as where a man runs up a large bill with only a slender probability of meeting it, or a larger bill than he can probably meet in full, or one of which he must defer the payment beyond a reasonable time. In all these cases, which are much aggravated, if the goods obtained are luxuries and not necessaries (for it is one of the plainest duties of every man, who is removed from absolute want, to live within his means), there is either actual dishonesty or a dangerous approximation to it, and it would be a great advance in every-day morality if society were to recognise this fact distinctly, and apportion its censures accordingly. Where the tradesman knows that he is running a risk, the customer being also aware that he knows it, and adapts his charges to the fact, it is a case of 'Greek meet Greek,' and, even if the customer deserves reprobation, the tradesman certainly deserves no compassion. But this is a case outside the range of honest dealing altogether, and must be regulated by other sentiments and other laws than those which prevail in ordinary commerce. There is another well-known, and to many men only too familiar, exception to the ordinary relation of debtor and creditor. A friend 'borrows' money of you, though it is understood on both sides that he will have no opportunity of repaying it, and that it is virtually a gift. Here, as the creditor does not expect any repayment, and the debtor knows that he does not, there is no act of dishonesty, but the debtor, by asking for a loan and not a gift, evades the obligation of gratitude and reciprocal service which would attach to the latter, and thus takes a certain advantage of his benefactor. In this case it would be far more straightforward, even if it involved some humiliation, to use plain words, and to accept at once the true position of a recipient, and not affect the seeming one of a borrower. Connected with the subject of debtor and creditor is the ungrounded notion, to which I have already adverted, that the payment of what are called debts of honour ought to take precedence of all other pecuniary obligations. As these 'debts of honour' generally arise from bets or play or loans contracted with friends, the position assumed is simply that debts incurred to members of our own class or persons whom we know place us under a greater obligation than debts incurred to strangers or persons belonging to a lower grade in society. As thus stated, the maxim is evidently preposterous and indefensible, and affords a good instance, as I have noticed in a previous chapter, of the subordination of the laws of general morality to the convenience and prejudices of particular cliques and classes. If there is any competition at all admissible between just debts, surely those which have been incurred in return for commodities supplied have a stronger claim than those, arising from play or bets, which represent no sacrifice on the part of the creditor.

Another instance of the class of cases which I am now considering is to be found in reckless gambling. Men who indulge in this practice are usually condemned as being simply hare-brained or foolish; but, if we look a little below the surface, we shall find that their conduct is often highly criminal. Many a time a man risks on play or a bet or a horse-race or a transaction on the stock exchange the permanent welfare, sometimes even the very subsistence, of his wife and children or others depending on him; or, if he loses, he cuts short a career of future usefulness, or he renders himself unable to develope, or perhaps even to retain, his business or his estates, and so involves his tenants, or clerks, or workmen in his ruin, or, perhaps, he becomes bankrupt and is thus the cause of wide-spread misery amongst his creditors. And, even if these extreme results do not follow, his rash conduct may be the cause of much minor suffering amongst his relatives or tradesmen or dependents, who may have to forego many legitimate enjoyments in consequence of his one act of greed or thoughtlessness, while, in all cases, he is encouraging by his example a practice which, if not his own ruin, is certain to be the ruin of others. The light-heartedness with which many a man risks his whole fortune, and the welfare of all who are dependent on him, for what would, if gained, be no great addition to his happiness, is a striking example of the frequent blindness of men to all results except those which are removed but one step from their actions. A gamester, however sanguine, sees that he may lose his money, but he does not see all the ill consequences to himself and others which the loss of his money will involve. Hence an act, which, if we look to the intention, is often only thoughtless, becomes, in result, criminal, and it is of the utmost importance that society, by its reprobation, should make men realise what the true nature of such actions is.

I pass now to a case of a different character, which has only, within recent years, begun to attract the attention of the moralist and politician at all--the peril to life and health ensuing on the neglect of sanitary precautions. A man carelessly neglects his drains, or allows a mass of filth to accumulate in his yard, or uses well-water without testing its qualities or ascertaining its surroundings. After a time a fever breaks out in his household, and, perhaps, communicates itself to his neighbours, the result being several deaths and much sickness and suffering. These deaths and this suffering are the direct result of his negligence, and, though it would, doubtless, be hard and unjust to call him a murderer, he is this in effect. Of course, if, notwithstanding warning or reflexion, he persists in his negligence, with a full consciousness of the results which may possibly ensue from it, he incurs a grave moral responsibility, and it is difficult to conceive a case more fit for censure, or even punishment. Nor are the members of a corporation or a board, in the administration of an area of which they have undertaken the charge, less guilty, under these circumstances, than is a private individual in the management of his own premises. If men were properly instructed in the results of their actions or pretermissions, in matters of this nature, and made fully conscious of the responsibility which those results entail upon them, there would soon be a marked decrease in physical suffering, disease, and premature deaths. The average duration of life, in civilized countries, has probably already been lengthened by the increased knowledge and the increased sense of responsibility which have even now been attained.

Closely connected with these considerations on the diminution of death, disease, and suffering by improved sanitary arrangements, is the delicate subject of the propagation of hereditary disease. It is a commonplace that the most important of all the acts of life, is that on which men and women venture most thoughtlessly. But experience shews, unmistakably, that there are many forms of disease, both mental and bodily, which are transmitted from the parents to the children, and that, consequently, the marriage of a diseased parent, or of a parent with a tendency to disease, will probably be followed by the existence of diseased children. In a matter of this kind, everything, of course, depends on the amount of the risk incurred, that is to say, on the extent of the evil and the probability of its transmission. The former of these data is supplied by common observation, the latter by the researches of the pathologist. It is for the moralist simply to draw attention to the subject, and to insist on the responsibility attaching to a knowledge of it. The marriages of persons who are very poor, and have no reasonable prospect of bringing up children in health, decency, and comfort, are open to similar considerations but, as in the last case, I must content myself with simply adverting to the responsibility attaching to them, and noting the extent to which that responsibility is usually ignored. In connexion with this question, it may be added that many of the attempts made by well-meaning people to alleviate poverty and distress have, unfortunately, too often the effect of ultimately aggravating those evils by diverting attention from their real causes. A not unnatural reluctance to discuss or reflect on matters of this delicate character, combined with the survival of maxims and sentiments derived from an entirely different condition of society, are, doubtless, to a great extent, the reasons of the backward condition of morality on this subject.

The importance, from a social point of view, of the careful education of children with reference to their future position in life has already been considered, but, in connexion with the class of duties I am now treating, I may draw attention to the obligation under which parents lie, in this respect, to their children themselves. The ancient morality, which was the product of the patriarchal form of society, when the ***patria potestas*** was still in vigour, laid peculiar stress on the duties of children to parents, while it almost ignored the reciprocal duties of parents to children. When the members of a family were seldom separated, and the pressure of population had not yet begun to be felt, this was the natural order of ideas with respect to the parental relation. But now that the common labour of the household is replaced by competition amongst individuals, and most young men and women have, at an early age, to leave their families and set about earning their own living, or carving out their own career, it is obvious, on reflexion, that parents are guilty of a gross breach of duty, if they do not use their utmost endeavours to facilitate the introduction of their children to the active work of life, and to fit them for the circumstances in which they are likely to be placed. To bring up a son or daughter in idleness or ignorance ought to be as great a reproach to a parent as it is to a child to dishonour its father or mother. And yet, in the upper and middle classes at all events, there are many parents who, without incurring much reprobation from their friends, prefer to treat their children like playthings or pet animals rather than to take the pains to train them with a view to their future trials and duties. It ought to be thoroughly realised, and, as the moral consciousness becomes better adapted to the existing circumstances of society, it is to be trusted that it will be realised, that parents have no moral right to do what they choose with their children, but that they are under a strict obligation both to society and to their children themselves so to mould their dispositions and develope their faculties and inform their minds and train their bodies as to render them good and useful citizens, and honest and skilful men. It is to be hoped that, some day, people will regard with as much surprise the notion that parents have a right to neglect the education of their children as we now regard with wonder, when we first hear of it; the maxim of archaic law, that a parent had a right to put his child to death.

    Much of the trouble, vexation, and misery of which men are the cause to themselves is due to cowardice, or the false shame which results from attaching undue importance to custom, fashion, or the opinion of others, even when that opinion is not confirmed by their own reflexion. Shame is an invaluable protection to men, as a restraining feeling. But the objects to which it properly attaches are wrongdoing, unkindness, discourtesy, to others, and, as regards ourselves, ignorance, imprudence, intemperance, impurity, and avoidable defects or misfortunes. While it confines itself to objects such as these, it is one of the sternest and, at the same time, most effective guardians of virtue and self-respect. But, as soon as a man begins to care about what others will say of circumstances not under his own control, such as his race, his origin, his appearance, his physical defects, or his lack of wealth or natural talents, he may be laying up for himself a store of incalculable misery, and is certainly enfeebling his character and impairing his chances of future usefulness. It is under the influence of this motive, for instance, that many a man lives above his income, not for the purpose of gratifying any real wants either of himself or his family, but for the sake of 'keeping up appearances,' though he is exposing his creditors to considerable losses, his family to many probable disadvantages, and himself to almost certain disgrace in the future. It is under the influence of this motive, too, that many men, in the upper and middle classes, rather than marry on a modest income, and drop out of the society of their fashionable acquaintance, form irregular sexual connexions, which are a source of injury to themselves and ruin to their victims.

A circumstance which has probably contributed largely, in recent times, to aggravate the feeling of false shame is the new departure which, in commercial communities, has been taken by class-distinctions. The old line, which formed a sharp separation between the nobility and all other classes, has been almost effaced, and in its place have been substituted many shades of difference between different grades of society, together with a broad line of demarcation between what may be called the genteel and the ungenteel classes. It was a certain advantage of the old line that it could not be passed, and, hence, though there might be some jealousy felt towards the nobility as a class, there were none of the heart-burnings which attach to an uncertain position or a futile effort to rise. In modern society, on the other hand, there is hardly any one whose position is so fixed, that he may not easily rise above or fall below it, and hence there is constant room for social ambition, social disappointment, and social jealousy. Again, the broad line of gentility, which now corresponds most closely with the old distinction of nobility, is determined by such a number of considerations,--birth, connexions, means, manners, education, with the arbitrary, though almost essential, condition of not being engaged in retail trade,--that those who are just excluded by it are apt to feel their position somewhat unintelligible, and, therefore, all the more galling to their pride and self-respect It would be curious to ascertain what proportion of the minor inconveniences and vexations of modern life is due to the perplexity, on the one side, and the soreness, on the other, created by the exclusiveness of class-distinctions. That these distinctions are an evil, in themselves, there can, I think, be no doubt. Men cannot, of course, all know one another, much less be on terms of intimacy with one another, and the degree of their acquaintance or intimacy will always be largely dependent on community of tastes, interests, occupations, and early associations. But these facts afford no reason why one set of men should look down with superciliousness and disdain on another set of men who have not enjoyed the same early advantages or are not at present endowed with the same gifts or accomplishments as themselves, or why they should hold aloof from them when there is any opportunity of common action or social intercourse. The pride of class is eminently unreasonable, and, in those who profess to believe in Christianity, pre-eminently inconsistent. It will always, probably, continue to exist, but we may hope that it will be progressively modified by the advance of education, by the spread of social sympathy, and by a growing habit of reflexion. The ideal social condition would be one in which, though men continued to form themselves into groups, no one thought the worse or the more lightly of another, because he belonged to a different group from himself.

Connected with exaggerated class-feeling are abuses of-esprit de corps. Unlike class-feeling, *esprit de corps* is, in itself, a good. It binds men together, as in a vessel or a regiment, a school or a college, an institution or a municipality, and leads them to sacrifice their ease or their selfish aims, and to act loyally and cordially with one another in view of the common interest. It is only when it sacrifices to the interests of its own body wider interests still, and subordinates patriotism or morality to the narrower sentiment attaching to a special law of honour, that it incurs the reprobation of the moralist. But that it does sometimes deservedly incur this reprobation, admits of no question. A man, to save the honour of his regiment, may impair the efficiency of an army, or, to promote the interests of his college or school, may inflict a lasting injury on education, or, to protect his associates, may withhold or pervert evidence, or, to aggrandize his trade, may ruin his country. It is the special province of the moralist, in these cases, to intervene, and point out how the more general is being sacrificed to the more special interest, the wider to the narrower sentiment, morality itself to a point of honour or etiquette. But, at the same time, he must recollect that the *esprit de corps* of any small aggregate of men is, as such, always an ennobling and inspiring sentiment, and that, unless it plainly detach them from the rest of the community, and is attended with pernicious consequences to society at large, it is unwise, if not reckless, to seek to impair it.

To descend to a subject of less, though still of considerable, importance, I may notice that cowardice and fear of 'what people will say' lies at the bottom of much ill-considered charity and of that facility with which men, often to the injury of themselves or their families, if not of the very objects pleaded for, listen to the solicitations of the inconsiderate or interested subscription-monger. It has now become a truism that enormous mischief is done by the indiscriminate distribution of alms to beggars or paupers. It is no less true, though not so obvious, that much unintentional harm is often done by subscriptions for what are called public objects. People ought to have sufficient mental independence to ask themselves what will be the ultimate effects of subscribing their money, and, if they honestly believe that those effects will be pernicious or of doubtful utility, they ought to have the courage to refuse it. There is no good reason, simply because a man asks me and I find that others are yielding to him, why I should subscribe a guinea towards disfiguring a church, or erecting an ugly and useless building, or extending pauperism, or encouraging the growth of luxurious habits, or spreading opinions which I do not believe. And I may be the more emboldened in my refusal, when I consider how mixed, or how selfish, are often the motives of those who solicit me, and that the love of notoriety, or the gratification of a feeling of self-importance, or a fussy restlessness, or the craving for preferment is frequently quite as powerful an incentive of their activity as a desire to promote the objects explicitly avowed. There is, moreover, an important consideration, connected with this subject, which often escapes notice, namely, the extent to which new and multiplied appeals to charity often interfere with older, nearer, and more pressing claims. Thus, the managers of the local hospital or dispensary or charity organisation have often too good cause to regret the enthusiastic philanthropy, which is sending help, of questionable utility, to distant parts of the world. People cannot subscribe to everything, and they are too apt to fall in with the most recent and most fashionable movement. In venturing on these remarks, I trust it is needless to say that I am far from deprecating the general practice of subscribing to charities and public objects, a form of co-operation which has been rendered indispensable by the habits and circumstances of modern life. I am simply insisting on the importance and responsibility of ascertaining whether the aims proposed are likely to be productive of good or evil, and deprecating the cowardice or listlessness which yields to a solicitation, irrespectively of the merits of the proposal.

These solicitations often take the offensive form, which is intentionally embarrassing to the person solicited, of an appeal to relieve the purveyor of the subscription-list himself from the obligation incurred by a 'guarantee.' The issue is thus ingeniously and unfairly transferred from the claims of the object, which it is designed to promote, to the question of relieving a friend or a neighbour from a heavy pecuniary obligation. 'Surely you will never allow me to pay all this money myself.' But why not, unless I approve of the object, and, even if I do, why should I increase my subscription, on account of an obligation voluntarily incurred by you, without any encouragement from me? In a case of this kind, the 'guarantee' ought to be regarded as simply irrelevant, and the question decided solely on the merits of the result to be attained. Of course, I must be understood to be speaking here only of those cases in which the 'guarantee' is used as an additional argument for eliciting subscriptions, not of those cases in which, for convenience sake, or in order to secure celerity of execution, a few wealthy persons generously advance the whole sum required for a project, being quite willing to pay it themselves, unless they meet with ready and cheerful co-operation.

In the department of social intercourse, there are several applications of existing moral principles, and specially of the softer virtues of kindness, courtesy, and consideration for others, the observance of which would sensibly sweeten our relations to our fellow-men and, to persons of a sensitive temperament, render life far more agreeable and better worth living than it actually is. A few of these applications I shall attempt to point out. Amongst savage races, and in the less polished ranks of civilized life, men who disagree, or have any grudge against one another, resort to physical blows or coarse invective. In polite and educated circles, these weapons are replaced by sarcasm and innuendo. There are, of course, many advantages gained by the substitution of this more refined mode of warfare, but the mere fact that the intellectual skill which it displays gives pleasure to the bystanders, and wins social applause, renders its employment far more frequent than, on cool reflexion, could be justified by the occasions for it. There can be no doubt that it gives pain, often intense pain, especially where the victim is not ready enough to retaliate effectively in kind. And there can be no more justification for inflicting this peculiar kind of pain than any other, unless the circumstances are such as to demand it. Any one, who will take the trouble to analyse his acts and motives, will generally find, when he employs these weapons, that he is actuated not so much by any desire to reform the object of his attack or to deter, by these means, him or others from wrong-doing, as by a desire to show off his own cleverness and to leave behind him a mark of his power in the smart which he inflicts. These unamiable motives are least justifiable, when the victim is a social inferior, or a person who, by his age or position, is unable to retaliate on equal terms. To vanity and cruelty are then added cowardice, and, though all these vices may only be displayed on a very small scale, they are none the less really present. It may be laid down, however difficult, with our present social habits, it may be to keep the rule, that sarcasm should never be employed, except deliberately, and as a punishment, and that for innuendo, if justifiable by facts, men should always have the courage to substitute direct assertion.

Of the minor social vices, one of the commonest is a disregard, in conversation, of other persons' feelings. Men who lay claim to the character of gentlemen are specially bound to shew their tact and delicacy of feeling by avoiding all subjects which have a disagreeable personal reference or are likely to revive unpleasant associations in the minds of any of those who are present. And yet these are qualities which are often strangely conspicuous by their absence even in educated and cultivated society. One of the most repulsive and least excusable forms which this indifference to other persons' feelings takes is in impertinent curiosity. There are some people who, for the sake of satisfying a purposeless curiosity, will ask questions which they know it cannot be agreeable to answer. In all cases, curiosity of this kind is evidence of want of real refinement, and is a breach of the finer rules of social morality; but, when the questions asked are intended to extract, directly or indirectly, unwilling information on a man's private life or circumstances, they assume the character of sheer vulgarity. A man's private affairs, providing his conduct of them does not injuriously affect society, are no one's business but his own, and much pain and vexation of the smaller kind would be saved, if this very plain fact were duly recognised in social intercourse.

It may be noticed in passing, that there still lingers on in society a minor form of persecution, a sort of inquisition on a small scale, which consists in attempting to extract from a man a frank statement of his religious, social, or political opinions, though it is known or suspected all the time, that, if he responds to the invitation, it will be to his social or material disadvantage. In cases of this kind, it becomes a casuistical question how far a man is called on to disclose his real sentiments at the bidding of any impertinent questioner. That the free expression of opinion should be attended with this danger is, of course, a proof how far removed we still are from perfect intellectual toleration.

Impertinent curiosity is offensive, not only because it shews an indifference to the feelings of the person questioned, but because it savours of gratuitous interference in his affairs. This quality it shares with another of the minor social vices, the tendering of unasked for advice, or, in brief, impertinent advice. There are certain circumstances and relations in which men have the right, even if they are not under the obligation, to give unsolicited advice, as where a man is incurring an unknown danger or foregoing some unsuspected advantage, or to their servants, or children, or wards, or pupils; but, in all these cases, either the special circumstance or the special relation implies superiority of knowledge or superiority of position on the part of the person tendering the advice, and to assume this superiority, where it does not plainly exist, is an act of impertinence. Just as the assumption of superiority wounds a man's self-respect, so does the disposition to meddle in his affairs, which is generally founded on that assumption, affect his sense of independence, and, hence, an act which includes both grounds of offence seems to be a peculiarly legitimate object of resentment. The lesson of letting other people alone is one which men are slow to learn, though there are few who, in their own case, do not resent any attack on their liberty of judgment or action. This is emphatically one of the cases in which we should try to put ourselves in the place of others, and act to them as we would that they should act towards us.

Excessive, and often ill-natured, criticism of others is one of the minor vices which seem to grow up with advancing civilisation and intelligence rather than to retreat before them. It seems, as a rule, to prevail much more in educated than in uneducated society. The reason is not difficult to find. Education naturally makes men more fastidious and more keenly alive to the defects of those with whom they associate. And then, when educated men converse together, they are apt, merely from the facility with which they deal with language, to express in an exaggerated form the unfavourable estimate which they have formed of others, especially if this exaggerated form can be compressed into an epigram. But it requires little reflexion to see that this keen and exaggerated habit of criticism must be productive of much discomfort in a society in which it is general, and that, when applied to literary work, even though it may be a protection against inaccuracy and breaches of taste, it must be a great discouragement to the young and repressive of much honest and valuable effort. To restrain the critical spirit, whether applied to mind or conduct, with proper limits, it is necessary, keeping these considerations in view, to ask how much we can reasonably or profitably require of men, and, above all, never to lose that sympathetic touch with others which renders us as keenly alive to their difficulties as their errors, to their aspirations as their failure to fulfil them.

I shall say nothing here of detraction, backbiting, or malicious representation, because these are social vices which are too obvious and too generally acknowledged to be of any service as illustrations of those extensions or new applications of morality which I have in view in the present chapter. I may, however, notice in passing, that the invention or exaggeration of stories, which have a tendency to bring men into ridicule or contempt, is a practice which, from the entertainment it affords, is too easily tolerated by society, and usually fails to meet with the reprobation it deserves.

I shall advert to only one other topic, namely, the treatment of the lower animals. With rare exceptions, it is only of late that this subject has been regarded as falling within the sphere of ethics, and it is greatly to the credit of Bentham that he was amongst the first to recognise its importance and to commend it to the consideration of the legislator. That the lower animals, as sentient beings, have a claim on our sympathies, and that, consequently, we have duties in respect of them, I can no more doubt than that we have duties in respect to the inferior members of our own race. But, at the same time, considering their place in the economy of nature, I cannot doubt that man has a right, within certain limits, to use them, and even to kill them, for his own advantage. What these limits are is a question by no means devoid of difficulty. There are those who maintain that we have no right to kill animals for food, while there are those who, without maintaining this extreme position, hold that we have no right to cause them pain for the purposes of our own amusement, or even for the alleviation of human suffering by means of the advancement of physiological and medical science. It will be seen that the three questions here raised are the legitimacy of the use of animal food, of field sports, and of vivisection. As respects the first, I do not doubt that, considering their relative places in the scale of being, man is morally justified in sacrificing the lives of the lower animals to the maintenance of his own health and vigour, let alone the probability that, if he did not, they would multiply to such an extent as to endanger his existence, and would themselves, in the aggregate, experience more suffering from the privation caused by the struggle for life than they now do by incurring violent deaths. At the same time, though man may kill the lower animals for his own convenience, he is bound not to inflict needless suffering on them. The torture of an animal, for no adequate purpose, is absolutely indefensible. Cock-fights, bull-fights, and the like seem to me to admit of no more justification than the gladiatorial shows. Are field-sports, then, in the same category? The answer, I think, depends on three considerations: (1) would the animal be killed any way, either for food, or as a beast of prey; (2) what is the amount of suffering inflicted on it, in addition to that which would be inflicted by killing it instantaneously; (3) for what purpose is this additional suffering inflicted. I shall not attempt to apply these considerations in detail, but I shall simply state as my opinion that, amongst the results of a legitimate application of them, would be the conclusions that worrying a dog or a cat is altogether unjustifiable; that fox-hunting might be justified on the ground that the additional suffering caused to the fox is far more than counterbalanced by the beneficial effects, in health and enjoyment, to the hunter; that shooting, if the sportsman be skilful, is one of the most painless ways of putting a bird or a stag to death, and, therefore, requires no justification, whereas, if the sportsman be unskilful, the sufferings which he is liable to cause, through a lingering and painful death, ought to deter him from practising his art. With regard to the much-debated question of vivisection, it seems to me utterly untenable, and eminently inconsistent on the part of those who eat animal food or indulge in field-sports, to maintain that, under no circumstances, is it morally justifiable to inflict pain on the lower animals for the purpose of ascertaining the causes or remedies of disease. But, having once made this admission, I should insist on the necessity of guarding it by confining the power of operating on the living animal to persons duly authorised, and by limiting it to cases of research as distinct from demonstration. Those, moreover, who are invested with this serious responsibility, ought to feel morally bound to inflict no superfluous suffering, and ought, consequently, to employ anaesthetics, wherever they would not unduly interfere with the conduct of the experiment; to resort, as far as possible, to the lower rather than the higher organisms, as being less susceptible of pain; and to limit their experiments, both in number and duration, as far as is consistent with the objects for which they are permitted to perform them. This whole question, however, of our relation to the lower animals is one which is fraught with much difficulty, and supplies a good instance of the range of subjects within which the moral sentiment is probably in the course of development. Recent researches, and, still more, recent speculations, have tended to impress us with the nearness of our kinship to other animals, and, hence, our sympathies with them and our interest in their welfare have been sensibly quickened. The word philanthropy no longer expresses the most general of the sympathetic feelings, and we seem to require some new term which shall denote our fellow-feeling with the whole sentient creation.

Such is a sample, and I must repeat that it is intended only as a sample, of the class of questions to which, as it seems to me, the moral test still admits of further application. Morality, or the science and art of conduct, had its small beginnings, I conceive, in the primeval household and has only attained its present grand proportions by gradual increments, derived partly from the semi-conscious operations of the human intelligence adapting itself to the circumstances in which it is placed, partly from the conscious meditations of reflective men. That it is likely to advance in the future, as it has done in the past, notwithstanding the many hindrances to its progress which confessedly exist, is, I think, an obvious inference from experience. We may not unreasonably hope that there will be a stricter sense of justice, a more complete realisation of duty, more delicacy of feeling, a greater refinement of manners, more kindliness, quicker and wider sympathies in the coming generations than there are amongst ourselves. I have attempted, in this Essay, briefly to delineate the nature of the feelings on which this progress depends, and of the considerations by which it is guided, as well as to indicate some few out of the many directions which it is likely to take in the future. In the former part of my task, I am aware that I have run counter to many prejudices of long standing, and that the theories which I consider to be alone consistent with the fact of the progress of morality, may by some be thought to impair its authority. But if morality has its foundations in the constitution of human nature, which itself proceeds from the Divine Source of all things, I conceive that its credentials are sufficiently assured. In the present chapter, I have, in attempting to illustrate the possibility of future improvements in the art and theory of conduct, been necessarily led to note some deficiencies in the existing moral sentiment. This is always an unwelcome and invidious task. Men do not like to be reminded of their moral failings, and there is hardly any man, however critical he may be of others, who, in the actual conduct of life, does not appear to delude himself with the idea that his own moral practice is perfect. I appeal, however, from the unconscious assumptions of men to their powers of reflexion, and I ask each man who reads this book to consider carefully within himself whether, on the principles here set out, much of the conduct and many of the ethical maxims which are now generally accepted do not admit of refinement and improvement. In the sphere of morals, as in all other departments of human activity, we are bound to do for our successors what our predecessors were bound to do, and mostly did, for us--transmit the heritage we have received with all the additions and adaptations which the new experiences and changing conditions of life have rendered necessary or desirable.

www.bookjungle.com *email: sales@bookjungle.com fax: 630-214-0564 mail: Book Jungle PO Box 2226 Champaign, IL 61825*

The Codes Of Hammurabi And Moses
W. W. Davies

QTY

The discovery of the Hammurabi Code is one of the greatest achievements of archaeology, and is of paramount interest, not only to the student of the Bible, but also to all those interested in ancient history...

Religion **ISBN:** *1-59462-338-4* *Pages:*132
MSRP $12.95

The Theory of Moral Sentiments
Adam Smith

QTY

This work from 1749. contains original theories of conscience amd moral judgment and it is the foundation for systemof morals.

Philosophy **ISBN:** *1-59462-777-0* *Pages:*536
MSRP $19.95

Jessica's First Prayer
Hesba Stretton

QTY

In a screened and secluded corner of one of the many railway-bridges which span the streets of London there could be seen a few years ago, from five o'clock every morning until half past eight, a tidily set-out coffee-stall, consisting of a trestle and board, upon which stood two large tin cans, with a small fire of charcoal burning under each so as to keep the coffee boiling during the early hours of the morning when the work-people were thronging into the city on their way to their daily toil...

Childrens **ISBN:** *1-59462-373-2* **Pages:**84
MSRP $9.95

My Life and Work
Henry Ford

QTY

Henry Ford revolutionized the world with his implementation of mass production for the Model T automobile. Gain valuable business insight into his life and work with his own auto-biography... "We have only started on our development of our country we have not as yet, with all our talk of wonderful progress, done more than scratch the surface. The progress has been wonderful enough but..."

Biographies/ **ISBN:** *1-59462-198-5* **Pages:**300
MSRP $21.95

www.bookjungle.com email: sales@bookjungle.com fax: 630-214-0564 mail: Book Jungle PO Box 2226 Champaign, IL 61825

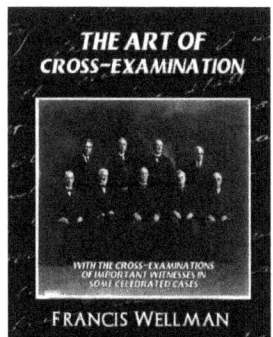

The Art of Cross-Examination
Francis Wellman

QTY

I presume it is the experience of every author, after his first book is published upon an important subject, to be almost overwhelmed with a wealth of ideas and illustrations which could readily have been included in his book, and which to his own mind, at least, seem to make a second edition inevitable. Such certainly was the case with me; and when the first edition had reached its sixth impression in five months, I rejoiced to learn that it seemed to my publishers that the book had met with a sufficiently favorable reception to justify a second and considerably enlarged edition. ..

Reference   ISBN: *1-59462-647-2*   Pages:412   MSRP *$19.95*

On the Duty of Civil Disobedience
Henry David Thoreau

QTY

Thoreau wrote his famous essay, On the Duty of Civil Disobedience, as a protest against an unjust but popular war and the immoral but popular institution of slave-owning. He did more than write—he declined to pay his taxes, and was hauled off to gaol in consequence. Who can say how much this refusal of his hastened the end of the war and of slavery ?

Law   ISBN: *1-59462-747-9*   Pages:48   MSRP *$7.45*

Dream Psychology Psychoanalysis for Beginners
Sigmund Freud

QTY

Sigmund Freud, born Sigismund Schlomo Freud (May 6, 1856 - September 23, 1939), was a Jewish-Austrian neurologist and psychiatrist who co-founded the psychoanalytic school of psychology. Freud is best known for his theories of the unconscious mind, especially involving the mechanism of repression; his redefinition of sexual desire as mobile and directed towards a wide variety of objects; and his therapeutic techniques, especially his understanding of transference in the therapeutic relationship and the presumed value of dreams as sources of insight into unconscious desires.

Psychology   ISBN: *1-59462-905-6*   Pages:196   MSRP *$15.45*

The Miracle of Right Thought
Orison Swett Marden

QTY

Believe with all of your heart that you will do what you were made to do. When the mind has once formed the habit of holding cheerful, happy, prosperous pictures, it will not be easy to form the opposite habit. It does not matter how improbable or how far away this realization may see, or how dark the prospects may be, if we visualize them as best we can, as vividly as possible, hold tenaciously to them and vigorously struggle to attain them, they will gradually become actualized, realized in the life. But a desire, a longing without endeavor, a yearning abandoned or held indifferently will vanish without realization.

Self Help   ISBN: *1-59462-644-8*   Pages:360   MSRP *$25.45*

www.bookjungle.com email: sales@bookjungle.com fax: 630-214-0564 mail: Book Jungle PO Box 2226 Champaign, IL 61825

QTY

	Title	ISBN	Price
☐	**The Rosicrucian Cosmo-Conception Mystic Christianity** by *Max Heindel* *The Rosicrucian Cosmo-conception is not dogmatic, neither does it appeal to any other authority than the reason of the student. It is: not controversial, but is: sent forth in the, hope that it may help to clear..*	ISBN: *1-59462-188-8* New Age/Religion Pages 646	**$38.95**
☐	**Abandonment To Divine Providence** by *Jean-Pierre de Caussade* *"The Rev. Jean Pierre de Caussade was one of the most lively spiritual writers of the Society of Jesus in France in the 18th Century. His death took place at Toulouse in 1751. His works have gone through many editions and have been republished..."*	ISBN: *1-59462-228-0* Inspirational/Religion Pages 400	**$25.95**
☐	**Mental Chemistry** by *Charles Haanel* *Mental Chemistry allows the change of material conditions by combining and appropriately utilizing the power of the mind. Much like applied chemistry creates something new and unique out of careful combinations of chemicals the mastery of mental chemistry...*	ISBN: *1-59462-192-6* New Age Pages 354	**$23.95**
☐	**The Letters of Robert Browning and Elizabeth Barret Barrett 1845-1846 vol II** by *Robert Browning* and *Elizabeth Barrett*	ISBN: *1-59462-193-4* Biographies Pages 596	**$35.95**
☐	**Gleanings In Genesis (volume I)** by *Arthur W. Pink* *Appropriately has Genesis been termed "the seed plot of the Bible" for in it we have, in germ form, almost all of the great doctrines which are afterwards fully developed in the books of Scripture which follow...*	ISBN: *1-59462-130-6* Religion/Inspirational Pages 420	**$27.45**
☐	**The Master Key** by *L. W. de Laurence* *In no branch of human knowledge has there been a more lively increase of the spirit of research during the past few years than in the study of Psychology, Concentration and Mental Discipline. The requests for authentic lessons in Thought Control, Mental Discipline and...*	ISBN: *1-59462-001-5* New Age/Business Pages 422	**$30.95**
☐	**The Lesser Key Of Solomon Goetia** by *L. W. de Laurence* *This translation of the first book of the "Lemegton" which is now for the first time made accessible to students of Talismanic Magic was done, after careful collation and edition, from numerous Ancient Manuscripts in Hebrew, Latin, and French...*	ISBN: *1-59462-092-X* New Age/Occult Pages 92	**$9.95**
☐	**Rubaiyat Of Omar Khayyam** by *Edward Fitzgerald* *Edward Fitzgerald, whom the world has already learned, in spite of his own efforts to remain within the shadow of anonymity, to look upon as one of the rarest poets of the century, was born at Bredfield, in Suffolk, on the 31st of March, 1809. He was the third son of John Purcell...*	ISBN: *1-59462-332-5* Music Pages 172	**$13.95**
☐	**Ancient Law** by *Henry Maine* *The chief object of the following pages is to indicate some of the earliest ideas of mankind, as they are reflected in Ancient Law, and to point out the relation of those ideas to modern thought.*	ISBN: *1-59462-128-4* Religion/History Pages 452	**$29.95**
☐	**Far-Away Stories** by *William J. Locke* *"Good wine needs no bush, but a collection of mixed vintages does. And this book is just such a collection. Some of the stories I do not want to remain buried for ever in the museum files of dead magazine-numbers an author's not unpardonable vanity..."*	ISBN: *1-59462-129-2* Fiction Pages 272	**$19.45**
☐	**Life of David Crockett** by *David Crockett* *"Colonel David Crockett was one of the most remarkable men of the times in which he lived. Born in humble life, but gifted with a strong will, an indomitable courage, and unremitting perseverance...*	ISBN: *1-59462-250-7* Biographies/New Age Pages 424	**$27.45**
☐	**Lip-Reading** by *Edward Nitchie* *Edward B. Nitchie, founder of the New York School for the Hard of Hearing, now the Nitchie School of Lip-Reading, Inc, wrote "LIP-READING Principles and Practice". The development and perfecting of this meritorious work on lip-reading was an undertaking...*	ISBN: *1-59462-206-X* How-to Pages 400	**$25.95**
☐	**A Handbook of Suggestive Therapeutics, Applied Hypnotism, Psychic Science** by *Henry Munro*	ISBN: *1-59462-214-0* Health/New Age/Health/Self-help Pages 376	**$24.95**
☐	**A Doll's House: and Two Other Plays** by *Henrik Ibsen* *Henrik Ibsen created this classic when in revolutionary 1848 Rome. Introducing some striking concepts in playwriting for the realist genre, this play has been studied the world over.*	ISBN: *1-59462-112-8* Fiction/Classics/Plays 308	**$19.95**
☐	**The Light of Asia** by *sir Edwin Arnold* *In this poetic masterpiece, Edwin Arnold describes the life and teachings of Buddha. The man who was to become known as Buddha to the world was born as Prince Gautama of India but he rejected the worldly riches and abandoned the reigns of power when...*	ISBN: *1-59462-204-3* Religion/History/Biographies Pages 170	**$13.95**
☐	**The Complete Works of Guy de Maupassant** by *Guy de Maupassant* *"For days and days, nights and nights, I had dreamed of that first kiss which was to consecrate our engagement, and I knew not on what spot I should put my lips..."*	ISBN: *1-59462-157-8* Fiction/Classics Pages 240	**$16.95**
☐	**The Art of Cross-Examination** by *Francis L. Wellman* *Written by a renowned trial lawyer, Wellman imparts his experience and uses case studies to explain how to use psychology to extract desired information through questioning.*	ISBN: *1-59462-309-0* How-to/Science/Reference Pages 408	**$26.95**
☐	**Answered or Unanswered?** by *Louisa Vaughan* Miracles of Faith in China	ISBN: *1-59462-248-5* Religion Pages 112	**$10.95**
☐	**The Edinburgh Lectures on Mental Science (1909)** by *Thomas* *This book contains the substance of a course of lectures recently given by the writer in the Queen Street Hall, Edinburgh. Its purpose is to indicate the Natural Principles governing the relation between Mental Action and Material Conditions...*	ISBN: *1-59462-008-3* New Age/Psychology Pages 148	**$11.95**
☐	**Ayesha** by *H. Rider Haggard* *Verily and indeed it is the unexpected that happens! Probably if there was one person upon the earth from whom the Editor of this, and of a certain previous history, did not expect to hear again...*	ISBN: *1-59462-301-5* Classics Pages 380	**$24.95**
☐	**Ayala's Angel** by *Anthony Trollope* *The two girls were both pretty, but Lucy who was twenty-one who supposed to be simple and comparatively unattractive, whereas Ayala was credited, as her Bombwhat romantic name might show, with poetic charm and a taste for romance. Ayala when her father died was nineteen...*	ISBN: *1-59462-352-X* Fiction Pages 484	**$29.95**
☐	**The American Commonwealth** by *James Bryce* *An interpretation of American democratic political theory. It examines political mechanics and society from the perspective of Scotsman James Bryce*	ISBN: *1-59462-286-8* Politics Pages 572	**$34.45**
☐	**Stories of the Pilgrims** by *Margaret P. Pumphrey* *This book explores pilgrims religious oppression in England as well as their escape to Holland and eventual crossing to America on the Mayflower, and their early days in New England...*	ISBN: *1-59462-116-0* History Pages 268	**$17.95**

www.bookjungle.com *email:* sales@bookjungle.com *fax:* 630-214-0564 *mail:* Book Jungle PO Box 2226 Champaign, IL 61825

QTY

The Fasting Cure *by Sinclair Upton* ISBN: *1-59462-222-1* **$13.95**
In the Cosmopolitan Magazine for May, 1910, and in the Contemporary Review (London) for April, 1910, I published an article dealing with my experiences in fasting. I have written a great many magazine articles, but never one which attracted so much attention... New Age/Self Help/Health Pages 164

Hebrew Astrology *by Sepharial* ISBN: *1-59462-308-2* **$13.45**
In these days of advanced thinking it is a matter of common observation that we have left many of the old landmarks behind and that we are now pressing forward to greater heights and to a wider horizon than that which represented the mind-content of our progenitors... Astrology Pages 144

Thought Vibration or The Law of Attraction in the Thought World ISBN: *1-59462-127-6* **$12.95**
by William Walker Atkinson Psychology/Religion Pages 144

Optimism *by Helen Keller* ISBN: *1-59462-108-X* **$15.95**
Helen Keller was blind, deaf, and mute since 19 months old, yet famously learned how to overcome these handicaps, communicate with the world, and spread her lectures promoting optimism. An inspiring read for everyone... Biographies/Inspirational Pages 84

Sara Crewe *by Frances Burnett* ISBN: *1-59462-360-0* **$9.45**
In the first place, Miss Minchin lived in London. Her home was a large, dull, tall one, in a large, dull square, where all the houses were alike, and all the sparrows were alike, and where all the door-knockers made the same heavy sound... Childrens/Classic Pages 88

The Autobiography of Benjamin Franklin *by Benjamin Franklin* ISBN: *1-59462-135-7* **$24.95**
The Autobiography of Benjamin Franklin has probably been more extensively read than any other American historical work, and no other book of its kind has had such ups and downs of fortune. Franklin lived for many years in England, where he was agent... Biographies/History Pages 332

Name	
Email	
Telephone	
Address	
City, State ZIP	

☐ Credit Card   ☐ Check / Money Order

Credit Card Number	
Expiration Date	
Signature	

Please Mail to: Book Jungle
  PO Box 2226
  Champaign, IL 61825
or Fax to: 630-214-0564

ORDERING INFORMATION
web: *www.bookjungle.com*
email: *sales@bookjungle.com*
fax: *630-214-0564*
mail: *Book Jungle PO Box 2226 Champaign, IL 61825*
or PayPal *to sales@bookjungle.com*

Please contact us for bulk discounts

DIRECT-ORDER TERMS

20% Discount if You Order Two or More Books
Free Domestic Shipping!
Accepted: Master Card, Visa, Discover, American Express

www.ingramcontent.com/pod-product-compliance
Lightning Source LLC
Chambersburg PA
CBHW081325040426
42453CB00013B/2306